What was the dinosaurs' favorite newspaper?
The Prehistoric Times!

What do you get when you cross a Diplodocus with a computer?
A ten-ton know-it-all!

What do you call a dinosaur that's sleeping?
A Stegosnaurus!

1001 DINOSAUR JOKES FOR KIDS

Alice Saurus

BALLANTINE BOOKS • NEW YORK

Sale of this book without a front cover may be unauthorized. If this book is coverless, it may have been reported to the publisher as "unsold or destroyed" and neither the author nor the publisher may have received payment for it.

Copyright © 1993 by Dora Wood

All rights reserved under International and Pan-American Copyright Conventions. Published in the United States of America by Ballantine Books, a division of Random House, Inc., New York, and simultaneously in Canada by Random House of Canada Limited, Toronto.

Library of Congress Catalog Card Number: 93-90181

ISBN 0-345-38496-2

Manufactured in the United States of America

First Edition: September 1993

Contents

Prehistoric Times	1
No Wonder They're Extinct	37
Never Cross a Dinosaur with a Skunk	80
Dino-mite!	114
Ask Me if I'm a Brontosaurus	128
The Lizard of Oz	163
Tyrannosaurus, My Foot	168

Acknowledgements

Thanks to my friends who told me jokes: Hector Leonardi, Mike Mahana, Peter Borland, Peter Halpert. I never forget good ole Charlie Pulaski. Hi to Dorothea Margaret and Matthew Albert.

Thanks, too, to my editor, Betsy Flagler, who laughs out loud.

1001 DINOSAUR JOKES FOR KIDS

The Prehistoric Times —The Crazy Ways of Dinosaurs

What do you call a dinosaur that's sleeping?
A Stegosnaurus!

What's bigger than a Tyrannosaurus?
Its appetite!

Why did dinosaurs have leather skins?
Because they'd have looked silly in wool!

What was the dinosaurs' favorite newspaper?
The Prehistoric Times!

What always followed a Brontosaurus?
Its tail!

What do you get if you cross a Tyrannosaurus with a glove?
I don't know—but don't stick your hand in it!

Why do thirsty dinosaurs always wear watches?
Because they have springs in them!

Did you hear about the Stegosaurus who did bird impressions?
It ate worms for breakfast!

Who gave the dinosaurs a dollar whenever they lost a tooth?
The Tooth Fairydactyl!

Why can't you send a telegram to a Diplodocus?
Because they're all dead!

Why did the Allosaurus carry a ruler to bed at night?
Because it wanted to know how long it had slept!

What do you get if you cross a Diplodocus with an encyclopedia?
A ten-ton know-it-all!

What did Ankylosaurus have that no other dinosaurs did?
Baby Ankylosaurus!

"Doctor, Doctor, I keep seeing Triceratops!"
"Have you seen an optometrist?"
"No, just more Triceratops!"

Two Pterydactyl watched as a comet raced across the sky.
"Boy," said one. "I wish I could fly that fast!"
"You would," said the other, "if your tail was on fire!"

Why is a Tyrannosaurus big, mean, and ugly?
Because if it were small, friendly, and cute it'd be a hamster!

Which is the hardest dinosaur to tame?
Bronco-saurus!

What kind of dinosaur is served in the finest restaurants?
Steak-osaurus!

If ten Stegosaurus are walking through a clearing, and an Allosaurus comes along and eats one, how many are left?
None. The others ran away!

Where does a Tyrannosaurus sit in a movie theater?
Wherever it wants!

Why wouldn't a Tyrannosaurus eat a lawyer?
Professional courtesy!

How do you run over a Brontosaurus?
Climb up its tail, dash along its back and up its neck, and then jump when you get to the head!

MOTHER PTERODACTYL: It's time for you to leave the nest. Go over to the edge and jump.
BABY PTERODACTYL: But what if I can't fly?
MOTHER PTERODACTYL: Then you'll be jumping to a conclusion!

How do you get down from a Diplodocus?
You don't. You get down from a goose!

On what side did a Stegosaurus have the most plates?
On the outside!

What kind of dinosaurs went putt-putt-putt?
The bad golfers!

A restaurant had a sign that said it served any kind of sandwich you could think of, so Smart Alec went in and said, "I'll have a fried Brontosaurus sandwich on a bagel."

A few minutes later the waiter came back and said, "I'm sorry, sir, but we're out of bagels."

What did the Allosaurus use to blow things up?
Dino-mite!

What kind of credit card does a Tyrannosaurus carry?
Dino's Club!

What's it called when a Brontosaurus gets a bruise?
A Dino-sore!

What did the Triceratops use to make electricity?
A Dino-mo!

What do you call a Pterodactyl magician?
A Dinosorcerer!

Did you hear about Bronto Stega Bronto?
It's a Saurority!

Where did Titanosaurus go to college?
At the Saurbonne!

What was a Diplodocus's favorite dessert?
Saurbet!

What was the most popular pre-historic antacid?
Bronto Seltzer!

What do you call a room filled with six dinosaurs?
Dangerous!

Why did the stupid dinosaur get fired from its job at the M&M factory?
It threw away all the Ws!

MOTHER: Johnnie, why did you put a snake in your sister's bed?
JOHNNIE: Because I couldn't find a dinosaur!

Who's the most famous Brontosaurus singer?
Dino Shore!

Where do Triceratops have dinner?
At the Dino-Mat!

What is a Brontosaurus's favorite TV show?
Dinosty!

Why did the Allosaurus eat yeast and shoe polish before it went to sleep?
Because it wanted to rise and shine!

Why didn't Tyrannosaurus eat clowns?
Because they taste funny!

SARAH: What are you doing?
BETH: Writing a letter to a dinosaur.
SARAH: Why are you writing so slow?
BETH: Because they can't read very fast!

LESTER: I won a dinosaur at the carnival.
POLLY: Where do you keep it?
LESTER: In the bathtub.
POLLY: What do you do when you need to take a bath?
LESTER: I blindfold it.

How do you divide ten apples among seven dinosaurs?
Make applesauce!

How many Stegosaurus can walk into an empty clearing?
One—after that, it's not empty!

In what ways are a napkin and a Triceratops alike?
Both are hard to keep on your lap!

How do you drop a dinosaur egg three feet without breaking it?
Hold it four feet off the floor. Drop it three feet, then catch it a foot from the floor.

"Janet," said Mr. Phelps. "If I lay one dinosaur egg in this box, and two in that box, how many will that be?"
"Come on," Janet said, "you can't lay dinosaur eggs!"

How do you stop a Tyrannosaurus from charging?
Take away its Dino's Club card!

Which dinosaur could jump higher than a mountain?
All of them, silly. Mountains can't jump!

What is a Brontosaurus after he's 100 days old?
101 days old!

Why did the Allosaurus float down the river on its back?
So it wouldn't get its Nikes wet.

If a dinosaur is born in Australia, migrates to India, then goes to Africa, and dies in Turkey, what is it?
Extinct.

What is dinosaur skin good for?
To keep the dinosaur from falling apart.

What's the difference between a Brontosaurus and a banana?
About 20,000 pounds!

Why didn't more dinosaurs go to college?
Most of them didn't finish high school!

Where do you find Pterodactyl?
Where you lost them!

How does an Allosaurus get out of a phone booth?
The same way it got in!

"Doctor, doctor, you've got to help my sister. She thinks she's a Triceratops!"
"How long has this been going on?"
"Ever since she hatched!"

What's the only thing worse than an elephant with a runny nose?
A Brontosaurus with a sore throat!

Do you know how to make a sculpture out of a dinosaur?
Just get a big block of marble and chip away anything that doesn't look like a dinosaur!

Why did the Stegosaurus sit on the marshmallow?
So it wouldn't fall into the hot chocolate!

Why did Allosaurus wear purple tennis shoes?
Because white ones got dirty too fast!

BRACHIOSAURUS #1: How do I tell a mushroom from a toadstool?
BRACHIOSAURUS #2: Eat some for dinner. If you wake up in the morning, they're mushrooms!

How do you raise a baby dinosaur?
Give it some stilts!

What did the Fabrosaurus say when the Tyrannosaurus came over the hill?
"Here comes a Tyrannosaurus."

How do you stop a Garudimimus from digging up your garden?
Put it in your neighbor's yard.

BILLY: I found a Lanasaurus yesterday.
CINDY: Did you take it to the zoo?
BILLY: I did, and then we went to the movies.

What kind of dinosaurs eat burritos?
Tyrannosaurus Mex.

What do you call a dinosaur that's been left out in the rain?
Stegosau-rust.

What do you call the game that Brontosaurus play when five of them get into a phone booth?
Squash.

What do you do if you're walking through a forest and you see an Ultrasaurus in the tree above you?
Get out of the way.

What do you call a Diplodocus with a million bucks?
A gold-blooded reptile.

How did the dinosaur pay its rent?
With a Tyrannosaurus Check.

What do you call a dinosaur from Prague?
A Tyrannosaurus Czech.

Did you hear about the Tyrannosaurus who ate its uncle's wife?
It was an aunt-eater.

Where does a fifty-five-ton Ultrasaurus sleep?
Anywhere it wants.

What do you call a dinosaur that's angry?
Whatever it wants.

TEACHER: What family does the Xenotarsosaurus belong to?
LOUISE: I didn't know anybody around here had one.

What kind of dinosaur could see just as well with its tail as with its eyes?
One that was asleep.

What did Triceratops wear jogging shoes for?
Running.

Why did the Gasosaurus climb a tree?
It thought it was a squirrel.

Why did the Brontosaurus cross the road?
It thought it was a chicken.

What do you say to a dinosaur with three heads?
"Hello, hello, hello."

What happened when the Diplodocus sat on a tack?
It got the point.

What happens whenever a Brontosaurus takes a bath?
The bathroom floods.

COP: I'm looking for a dinosaur with one eye called Jaws.
TOM: What's his other eye called?

COP: I'm looking for a dinosaur with a watch.
SUE: Wouldn't glasses be more useful?

Did you hear about the Stegosaurus that took a seat on the bus?
The police made it give it back.

Why did the Allosaurus eat the campfire?
It wanted a light snack.

Why did the Ceratosaurus walk around in circles?
It got its foot stuck in a gopher hole.

What did dinosaurs like to drink when lounging by the pool?
A dino-quiri!

Who was the greatest prehistoric explorer?
Dino Boone!

What ancient documents tell us so much about dinosaur life?
The Dino Sea Scrolls!

Which dinosaur had the biggest nose?
Cyrano de Brontoac!

What kind of plans did Stegosaurus use to build houses?
Dinograms!

What did an Allosaurus get when it went to the doctor?
A dinognosis!

What was a Triceratops's favorite kind of gem?
A dinoamond!

What do you call a Pteranodon's journal?
A dinory!

Who ruled the dinosaurs?
The Dinotator!

What was a Carnosaurus's favorite restaurant?
Bronto King!

TEACHER: If I have a mother dinosaur and a father dinosaur, how many dinosaurs do I have?
DORA: Two.
TEACHER: Correct. And if the mother dinosaur lays two eggs and they hatch, what do I have?
DORA: Twins.

What shouldn't you do if you see a green Tyrannosaurus?
Thump it to see if it's ripe!

What did the Tyrannosaurus eat after all its teeth were pulled out?
Its dentist.

What does a Tyrannosaurus weigh?
Between six and ten tons, depending on what it had for lunch.

Why did the Allosaurus gobble up a dozen light bulbs?
Because it was a light eater!

Which dinosaurs had their eyes nearest together?
The smallest.

Why were Triceratops terrible dancers?
Because they had two left feet!

Why did the Camptosaurus scratch itself?
No one else knew where it was itching!

How do you make a Stegosaurus stew?
Keep it waiting for two hours.

How can you tell a Leptoceratops from spaghetti?
The Leptoceratops doesn't slip off your fork!

What do you get if you cross a Tyrannosaurus with a goose?
A dinosaur that honks before it eats you!

What should you do with a hundred million-year-old dinosaur?
Throw it a really big birthday party!

What happened to the Nyasasaurus that crossed a four-leaf clover with poison ivy?
It had a rash of good luck!

What would you get if you crossed a woodpecker with a Velociraptor?
An animal that knocked before it ate you!

JENNY: I've got a new pet dinosaur. Would you like to come over and play with it?
HAYLEY: I don't know. Does it bite?
JENNY: That's what I'm trying to find out!

TEACHER: Sophia, can you name four different dinosaurs?
SOPHIA: Mother dinosaur, father dinosaur, and two babies.

Mikey was taking his Mussasaurus for a walk when a policeman stopped him.
"Does your dinosaur have a license?" the policeman asked.
"Don't be silly," Mikey said. "It isn't old enough to drive."

NORMAN: My teacher was mad because I didn't know where dinosaur fossils could be found.
MOTHER: Well, next time remember where you left them.

What goes thump, thump, thump, bang!
A dinosaur in a minefield.

MOTHER: If I had seven dinosaurs and gave you two, how many would I have left?
ALICE: I don't know.
MOTHER: Why not? Aren't you learning anything in school?
ALICE: Sure, but there we do all our math with apples and oranges.

How can you tell if a dinosaur has been in your refrigerator?
By the footprints in the butter.

What's the best way to keep a Brontosaurus from going through the eye of a needle?
Tie a knot in its tail.

How can you tell if you're in bed with a Tyrannosaurus Rex?
It has "TR" embroidered on its pajamas.

What time is it when a Stegosaurus sits on your television set?
Time to get a new TV.

ANN: What's the difference between a dinosaur and a matterbaby?
PETE: What's a matterbaby?
ANN: I didn't know you cared.

Why did the Brontosaurus paint its toenails red, green, and yellow?
So it could hide in the M&Ms.

POLICEMAN: I'm looking for a dinosaur with one leg called Skip.
DORA: What are its other legs called?

BABY TYRANNOSAURUS: Is it good manners to eat Allosaurus with your fingers?
MOTHER TYRANNOSAURUS: No, you should eat your fingers all by themselves.

FIRST STUPID DINOSAUR: Where did all these rocks come from?
SECOND STUPID DINOSAUR: The glaciers brought them.
FIRST STUPID DINOSAUR: Then where are the glaciers?
SECOND STUPID DINOSAUR: I guess they went back for more rocks.

Did you hear about the dinosaur who thought he was covered in gold paint?
It had a gilt complex!

REBECCA: Yesterday I opened my oven and there was a dinosaur inside, so I ran for my shotgun.
LISA: Did you hit it?
REBECCA: No, by the time I got back it was out of my range.

Why did the dinosaur sprinkle sugar on its pillow?
It wanted to have sweet dreams!

Why are Brontosaurus so slow to apologize?
It takes them a long time to swallow their pride.

What would you get if you crossed an Ultrasaurus with a chicken?
The biggest cluck in the world.

Mr. and Mrs. Sellosaurus had seven daughters. Each daughter had one brother. How many dinosaurs were in their family?
Ten. Two parents, seven daughters and one son.

What do you get when a Fabrosaurus sits on a box of cookies?
Cookie crumbs.

Is anyone safe when a man-eating Tyrannosaurus is on the loose?
Sure. Women and children.

Why did the Geranosaurus eat light bulbs?
It thought it was a bright idea.

What happened to the Compsosuchus when a sugar cube fell on its head?
It got a lump.

How can you get a Camarasaurus to fly?
Buy it an airplane ticket.

What's a Tyrannosaurus's favorite activity when it snows?
Sleighing.

Why didn't the Adasaurus want to use toothpaste?
Because its teeth weren't loose.

What kind of dinosaur do you get if someone steps on your foot?
Ankylosaurus.

Why did the Burglarosaurus take a bath before breaking out of jail?
To make a clean getaway.

What's the difference between a Tyrannosaurus and an egg?
Well, if you don't know, don't go grocery shopping.

Why was the dinosaur arrested for assault after it went to sleep?
Because it hit the hay.

Why was the dinosaur poet so poor?
Because rhyme doesn't pay.

Did you hear about the Anodontosaurus who swallowed a doorknob?
Its stomach kept turning.

Did you hear about the Camptosaurus who stared at its watch all day?
It got clock-eyed.

What has a long neck, weighs thirty tons, and is blue?
A Brontosaurus holding its breath.

Did you hear about the Ultrasaurus that was hit by the Wells Fargo wagon?
It was stage struck.

Why did the Pterodactyl wear green sneakers?
Because its red ones were in the wash.

What did the dinosaurs raise during the rainy season?
Umbrellas.

Why did the dinosaur use maize to hold its pants up?
Because it was in the corn belt.

Why couldn't the dinosaur living in Africa be buried in South America?
Because it was still alive.

What's worse than a Brontosaurus with a sore throat?
A Tyrannosaurus with a toothache.

What do you call a Stegosaurus that crosses a river twice but is still covered in mud?
A dirty double-crosser.

Did you hear about the Camptosaurus that got a damp letter?
It had postage dew.

Why do dinosaurs have flat feet?
From jumping out of trees.

Why is it dangerous to go into the jungle between one and three in the afternoon?
That's when the dinosaurs jump out of trees.

Why were all the cavemen so short?
They went into the jungle between one and three in the afternoon.

Is it true that a dinosaur won't eat you if you're carrying a baseball bat?
It all depends on how fast you're carrying the bat.

JOAN: That dinosaur at the zoo has a glass eye.
BILL: How do you know?
JOAN: It just came out in conversation.

How do you milk a dinosaur?
First, you get a very big bucket. . . .

ROBBY: I wish I had enough money to buy ten dinosaurs.
ANN: Why do you want *ten* dinosaurs?
ROBBY: I don't. I just wish I had the money.

What does a dinosaur do when it hurts its toe?
It calls a toe truck.

Which dinosaurs could jump higher than the Empire State Building?
All of them. The Empire State Building can't jump.

CLIFF: How do you like my dinosaur? It's so tame it'll eat off your hand.
SHERRY: That's what I'm afraid of.

ZOOKEEPER: Dr. Moore, I'm afraid your little girl is in trouble for feeding the rabbits here at the zoo.
DR. MOORE: What's wrong with that?
ZOOKEEPER: She was feeding them to the dinosaurs!

DORIS JEAN: What did the dinosaurs call small white cats?
ROBERT: I don't know.
DORIS JEAN: Kittens.

CHERYL: How did the dinosaur get to the hospital quickly?
CHARLIE: Beats me.
CHERYL: It stood in the middle of the freeway.

ROBERT: Why did the dinosaur put two quarters in its pillow?
DORIS JEAN: I can't imagine.
ROBERT: They were its sleeping quarters.

CHARLIE: What happened to Ray when he was stepped on by an Ultrasaurus?
CHERYL: Who knows?
CHARLIE: He became an X-Ray.

SHERRY: Why did the dinosaur cross the road?
CLIFF: I'm stumped.
SHERRY: It thought it was a chicken.

SHERRY: Why did the second dinosaur cross the road?
CLIFF: I still don't know.
SHERRY: It had a date with the first one.

CLIFF: Why did the third dinosaur cross the road?
SHERRY: Now *I* don't know.
CLIFF: It was the chicken's day off.

LAURA: What did the dinosaurs do after they drank all the water in America?
DORA: I don't know.
LAURA: They drank Canada Dry.

CLIFF: What do you get if you cross a Triceratops with a crow?
SHERRY: I give up.
CLIFF: A lot of broken telephone wires.

DORA: What did the Stegosaurus do to keep from getting seasick?
LAURA: That's tough.
DORA: It bolted its food.

HAYLEY: Where did the dinosaur take its sick ship?
DORA: I don't know.
HAYLEY: To the dock.

PETER: What would you get if you crossed a Brontosaurus with a kangaroo?
MATTHEW: I can't guess.
PETER: Great big holes all over Australia.

DORA: What would you get if you crossed a Tyrannosaurus with a penguin?
HAYLEY: Beats me.
DORA: I don't know either, but you wouldn't have to buy it a tuxedo.

CHARLIE: What's the best thing to do with a blue Allosaurus?
DOROTHY: I can't figure it out.
CHARLIE: Make it laugh.

MARGARET: What happened to the Carnosaurus that ate a goose?
NIM: I'm stumped.
MARGARET: It was feeling a little down in the mouth.

DOROTHY: What should you do if a dinosaur comes to the door with a trombone?
CHARLIE: I can't imagine.
DOROTHY: Tell it to blow.

What did the Brontosaurus say after the Tyrannosaurus bit off its tail?
"It won't be long now!"

"Doctor, Doctor, my dinosaur just swallowed a roll of film! What do I do?"
"Relax," said the sawbones. "Let's just see what develops."

How do you cure fleas on a dinosaur?
It depends on what's the matter with them.

Did you hear about the dinosaur that only ate fireflies?
They filled it with delight.

Julie went into a pet store. "Do you carry dinosaurs?" she asked the woman behind the counter.
"Are you kidding?" said the lady. "They must weigh a ton."

SALLY: How come your dinosaur is painted yellow?
HARRY: That's so it can sneak up on school buses.
SALLY: That's absurd. I've never seen a dinosaur sneaking up on a school bus.
HARRY: See, it works.

Which had more legs: one Tyrannosaurus or no Tyrannosaurus?
None. One Tyrannosaurus had four legs, but no Tyrannosaurus had more.

JULIE: My grandfather once cut the tail off a Carnosaurus.
KRISTEN: Wow! What happened?
JULIE: That was the end of him.

How do you know that dinosaurs run faster than chickens?
Ever hear of Kentucky Fried Dinosaur?

Eric called to his mother: "I'm going outside to play."
"Not with those holes in your shirt!"
"No, with my dinosaur."

"Whenever I'm down in the dumps I get myself a new book about dinosaurs," Greg said.
"Gosh," said Sarah, "I get mine at the library."

The teacher said to Janet, "If I gave you two dinosaurs today and three tomorrow, how many would you have?"
"None," said Janet.
"Wouldn't you have five?"
"No, silly. They'd be dead. Don't you know that dinosaurs are extinct?"

Why did the dinosaur rock star have to cancel his concert?
He had Bronto-itis.

What do you give a Brontosaurus with the hiccups?
Lots of room.

TEACHER: Norman, spell Brontosaurus.
NORMAN: B-r-o-n-t-o-s-a-u-r.
TEACHER: But what comes at the end?
NORMAN: The tail.

What did the Camptosaurus have when he dropped a boulder on his toe?
A saur foot.

How did Arthur become the king of the paleontologists?
He pulled the saur from the stone.

Did you hear about the Pterodactyl that got a job at Macy's?
It was a department-saur.

Did you hear about the prehistorical scandal?
It was a saurdid tale.

Where do the Bosnian dinosaurs live?
In Saurajevo.

What was a Triceratops's favorite fish?
The saurdine.

What kind of clothing did a female dinosaur in India wear?
A sauri.

What about one that lived in Malaysia?
A saurong.

What was a Pterodactyl's favorite soft drink?
Saursparilla.

What was the most common bread during the Jurassic period?
Saur dough.

What kind of party did Benny the Bronto's friends throw on his birthday?
A saurprise party.

GILES: I say, old man, how did you get that dinosaur over here from the States?
NILES: I brought it with me on the ship.
GILES: Must have been frightfully expensive, what?
NILES: Not a bit. I just had to pay a small saur-charge.

What did the Bronto take when it went on vacation to Maui?
His saurfboard.

Where did everyone go for their operations during the Triassic period?
To the saurgeon.

What have you got when twenty Triceratops are living in your dining room?
A saurplus.

Did you hear about the expert in Gallimimus-watching?
He specialized in saurveillance.

What were the polls called during the Cretaceous period?
Saurveys.

Did you hear about the Triceratops who went to live all by himself in the deep jungle? It'd heard the world was going to come to an end, so it stockpiled food and water, and it wouldn't let anyone come near its home.
It was a saurvivalist.

Did you hear about the terrible accident during the Jurassic period?
A volcano erupted in Japan, covering everything with ash and lava. Only one Pterodactyl remained. It was the lone saurvivor.

What did the dinosaurs in France say to each other every evening?
Bon saur.

What was Gus the Goofasaurus's favorite dessert?
Strawberry saurcake.

How did the dinosaur secretary take dictation?
In saur hand.

Did you hear that Gus the Goofasaurus got a job in a coffee shop?
He was a saur-order cook.

Why did Gus have to get glasses?
He was saur-sighted.

How did the Brontosaurus talk to each other over long distances?
By saur-wave radio.

Where did baby dinosaurs come from?
The staurk brought them.

Who was the great existentialist philosopher of the Triassic period?
Jean-Paul Saurtre.

Who was the most famous dissident writer of the Jurassic period?
Aleksandr Saurzhenitsyn.

What was the biggest prehistoric desert?
The Saurhara.

Who was the most infamous dancer of the Cretaceous period?
Saurome.

How did the dinosaurs in Japan say goodbye?
Sauronara.

Where could you find the great dinosaur detectives?
At Saurtland Yard.

And who was the smartest of them all?
Saurlock Holmes.

Did Ernest Hemingway ever write about dinosaurs?
Sure, in *The Saurs of Kilimanjaro*.

Have you heard the story about the dinosaur princess who was chased away from home and had to live with a bunch of short guys in the jungle?
Saur White and the Seven Dwarves.

Which dinosaurs had trunks?
The ones that went on vacation.

What's invisible and smells like a Stegosaurus?
A Tyrannosaurus burp.

What kind of dinosaur has four legs and flies?
A dead one.

"Is this the veterinarian?"
"Yes."
"You must come quickly. My Tyrannosaurus has just eaten my television set."
"I'll be there in one hour."
"What do I do until then?"
"Listen to the radio."

REBECCA: I would hate to have 288 dinosaurs.
SUSAN: Why?
REBECCA: That would be too gross.

No Wonder They're Extinct

A policeman was directing traffic on a busy street corner one day when a car went by with a dinosaur in the back seat. The cop hopped on his motorcycle and pulled the car over.

"Hey, buddy," he said. "Where are you going with that dinosaur?"

"Why, I'm taking him to the Natural History Museum," said the driver.

"Well, I guess that's okay," the cop said, and he let them go.

A few days later he was at the same corner when the car went by again with the dinosaur in the back seat, wearing sunglasses. The cop jumped on his motorcycle again and chased the car down.

"I thought you were taking that dinosaur to the Natural History Museum," the cop said.

"I did," said the driver. "And now I'm taking him to the beach!"

Joe was at a diner eating a hamburger when a Camptosaurus came in and sat down on the stool next to him. All of a sudden it reached over, grabbed his hamburger, and ate it!

"Hey," Joe said to the waiter. "Do you know that dinosaur just ate my hamburger?"

"I don't think so," said the waiter. "But if you hum a few bars, I might remember it!"

Mr. Fuddy was always making up illnesses, and his doctor was tired of it. So when he called and said he had a rash, she told him to take a bath in dinosaur milk!

Silly Mr. Fuddy went to the dairy and told the man at the counter that he needed twenty gallons of dinosaur milk for a bath.

"Pasteurized?" laughed the dairy man.

"No," said Mr. Fuddy. "Only up to my neck."

A dinosaur walked into an ice-cream parlor and ordered a cone that cost $1.00. It put a ten dollar bill down on the counter, and Buster decided to cheat him, and only gave him five dollars back in change.

But Buster was pretty curious about why there was a dinosaur in his ice-cream parlor, so he said, "We don't see too many dinosaurs in here."

"At five dollars for an ice cream cone," said the dinosaur, "I'm not surprised."

Two cavemen were hunting in the jungle when they came across a Tyrannosaurus. "Run!" shouted the first one as the dinosaur started to chase them.

"We can't run faster than this thing," his friend yelled.

"I don't have to," the first caveman shouted back. "I just have to run faster than you!"

Mrs. Jones came home from work and found her husband sitting at the kitchen table.

"Where's dinner?" she asked.

"You'll never believe this, but I made some meatloaf and a dinosaur came through that door and ate it."

"No wonder they're extinct."

On his way to the lake, a Brontosaurus met two Allosaurus, three Nodosaurus, and a Segisaurus. On the back of each of the Allosaurus there was one Pterodactyl. On the back of each Nodosaurus there were three Pterodactyl. And on the back of the Segisaurus there was a hippopotamus. How many animals were going to the lake?

Just the Brontosaurus. All the others were coming back from the lake.

The Tyrannosaurus saw a turtle near the watering hole. He walked over and stomped on it. A Triceratops saw it happen, and it said, "How come you stomped on that turtle?"

The Tyrannosaurus said, "Five years ago I came here for a drink, and when I bent over to get some water, that turtle bit me on the nose."

"The same turtle? Boy, you've got a great memory."

The Tyrannosaurus smiled. "Turtle recall."

The Tyrannosaurus walked up to the Stegosaurus and bellowed, "Who is the king of the jungle?"

"You are, o mighty Rex," said the Stegosaurus.

The Tyrannosaurus smiled and walked along until he came to a Triceratops. "Who is king of the jungle?" he yelled.

"You are, o mighty Rex," whimpered the Triceratops.

The Tyrannosaurus smiled again and stomped along until he came to the lake, where a Brontosaurus was eating.

"Who is king of the jungle?" he shouted.

The Brontosaurus looked down at him from atop his long neck, and very casually flicked his huge tail. He hit the Tyrannosaurus and knocked him into a tree.

The Tyrannosaurus picked himself up, shook his head, and said, "Gee, you don't have to get angry just because you don't know the answer."

The Smartosaurus called all the other dinosaurs together for an important announcement. "I have just discovered," she said, "that we will be extinct in ten billion years."

A Goofosaurus in the front row fainted dead away. After the other dinosaurs woke him back up, the Smartosaurus said, "What's wrong with you? We've got another ten billion years."

"Ten billion?" the Goofosaurus said. "That's a relief. I thought you said ten *million*."

Two Tyrannosaurus were feasting on a fresh kill.

"Should we divide it into six pieces or eight?" the first one asked.

"Oh, just six," said the second. "I don't think we can eat eight pieces."

The grocery-store manager looked up all of a sudden to see a Brontosaurus stick its head through the window and begin eating all the fruits and vegetables. In about five minutes, everything was gone, and the Brontosaurus ran off.

The police came quickly and began asking the manager questions.

"Can you describe it?"

"What do you mean? All Brontosaurus look alike."

"Well, what color were its eyes?"

"How should I know? It was wearing a mask!"

A man came to a psychiatrist's office riding a dinosaur.

"Wow," the shrink said. "You need help right away."

"I sure do," said the dinosaur. "Get this guy off my back."

The paleontologist went to see a psychiatrist. He didn't want therapy, he just wanted to have two questions answered. The shrink thought it was a little odd, but he agreed.

"First," said the paleontologist, "is it possible to be in love with a dinosaur?"

"Absolutely not," the psychiatrist said. "It is impossible."

"Okay," said the paleontologist. "Do you know anybody who wants to buy a very large engagement ring?"

A fat dinosaur passed a thin dinosaur in a clearing.

The fat dinosaur said, "From the looks of you there must have been a famine."

The thin dinosaur said, "Yes, and from the looks of you, I know what caused it."

A woman was walking through a casino and saw three men playing poker with a dinosaur.

"That's a pretty smart dinosaur," said the woman.

"Ah, he's not so smart," one of the men said. "Every time he gets a good hand, he wags his tail."

Little Billy went to see the Boston Brontos play the Toronto Triceratops in a doubleheader. When he came home he drank three glasses of water.

"What's the matter?" said his mother. "Didn't you have any Coke at the baseball game?"

"No," said Billy. "The home team lost the opener."

Sarah was writing a paper for school, and she went to her father for help. "Dad, what's the difference between *exasperation* and *aggravation*?"

"Let me show you," her dad said. He went to the telephone and dialed a number he had just made up. A man answered, and Sarah's father said, "Hello, is Sam the dinosaur there?"

"No," said the man. "You have the wrong number. Besides, dinosaurs are extinct. Don't you know better than to make prank phone calls?" And he hung up.

"See," said Sarah's dad. "That man was probably just annoyed. Let me show you what *aggravation* is." And he dialed the same number again. "Hello, is Sam the dinosaur there?"

"NO!" yelled the man at the other end. "I just told you not to make prank phone calls. You've got a lot of nerve, buddy." And he slammed the phone down.

"Now that man is aggravated," Sarah's dad said. "Let me show you what *exasperation* is." And he dialed the number a third time. When the man at the other end yelled "Hello!" Sarah's dad said, "Hi, this is Sam the dinosaur. Any messages for me?"

Johnny studied all week for his test on dinosaurs. When he got to school that day, he found that there were models of ten different dinosaurs in the front of the classroom. But each of the models was covered with a bag, so that only the legs and feet showed.

Johnny's teacher was sick that day, and there was a substitute. When the time for the test came, the substitute said, "You are supposed to look at each of these dinosaurs and identify them."

Johnny raised his hand. "Aren't you going to uncover the dinosaurs so we can look at them?"

"There's nothing in the lesson plan about uncovering the dinosaurs. You'll just have to look at the legs and feet."

Johnny looked at the legs, but they all looked the same to him. He tried and tried to tell the difference between them, but he couldn't. He knew this wasn't the way the test was supposed to be given.

Finally, he couldn't take it anymore. He crumpled up the paper, threw it at the substitute teacher, and stomped toward the door.

"Hey, you, what's your name?" the substitute yelled.

Johnny turned around, pulled his pants up to his knees and said, "You guess, buddy, you just guess!"

The caveman had two sons named Toward and Away. He wasn't a very good hunter, and everyday he went out hunting and came back with just a little bit of food. He always told his wife about the big dinosaur that had barely escaped from him, and she always just laughed. One day he decided to take his sons hunting in the jungle. He came home that night all alone.

"What happened?" said his wife.

"Well, we were walking along, and all of a sudden a Tyrannosaurus jumped out in front of us. It must have been thirty feet tall. It chased us, and it caught Toward and swallowed him in one gulp."

"That's horrible!" his wife cried.

"That's nothing. You should have seen the one that got Away!"

Alice was driving down a country road when her car stalled. She got out and tried to fix it, but nothing was working. Suddenly a dinosaur wearing a baseball cap walked up and said, "It's probably your fuel valve."

Alice was scared out of her wits, and she ran off down the road until she came to a farm. She told the farmer what had happened.

"Was it a Brontosaurus wearing a baseball cap?" the farmer asked.

"Why, yes," Alice said.

"Oh, I wouldn't listen to Petey. He doesn't know much about cars."

Two dinosaurs were on a bicycle race across Scandinavia. They came to a fork in the road, and a man waved them down.

"Hi," said the man. "I'm Latte, the last Lapp."

"Oh, boy," said the first dinosaur. "Let's hurry."

"Why?" said the second.

"Silly, don't you know that when you come to the last Lapp, you're near the Finnish line?"

A private was transferred to a new outfit in the army. His old sergeant sent a letter to his new commanding officer. It said, "Joe is a good soldier, but he has one problem. He gambles all the time."

The new officer looked at Joe and said, "I hear you're a problem gambler. I won't stand for that kind of thing. What kind of stuff do you bet on?"

"Anything," said Joe. "In fact, I'll bet you fifty dollars that you've got a dinosaur tattooed on your back."

"Let's see your money," the officer shouted. They each pulled out fifty dollars, and then the officer took his shirt off. There wasn't a dinosaur tattooed on his back. "Let that be a lesson to you," he told Joe.

Satisfied with himself, he called Joe's old sergeant. "I've cured that private of his gambling," he said. "He won't be so eager to gamble after the money he just lost to me." And he told the sergeant what had happened.

"Don't bet on it," the sergeant said. "He bet me a thousand dollars that he could get you to take your shirt off five minutes after he met you."

Billy was walking down the street when he saw a man standing next to a dinosaur with a big FOR SALE sign around its neck.

"How much for the dinosaur, mister?" Billy asked.

"This is a talking dinosaur," the man said. "And you can have him for five dollars."

"Hey, don't try to trick me. Dinosaurs can't talk."

Suddenly the dinosaur spoke. "Please buy me from this man, sir. He's very cruel. He never feeds me or takes me for a walk. I used to be the richest talking dinosaur in the world, but he stole all my money and spent it on video games. I have performed before three presidents, the king of Spain, and the Pope."

"Boy," said Billy. "He *can* talk. How come you want to sell him so cheap?"

"Because he's such a terrible liar," the man replied.

Frank opened his door and found Lila standing there with a dinosaur behind her. She came in, and the dinosaur followed her. It knocked over the TV, stepped on the Sega game, ate the cat, and started clawing a hole in the wall.

"I wish you had more control over your dinosaur," Frank said.

"My dinosaur?" said Lila. "I thought it was *your* dinosaur."

The phone rang at the police station, and Officer Tran picked it up.

"You've got to help me," said the man on the other end. "My dinosaur has run away."

"I'm sorry, sir, but you'll have to call the Humane Society. The police don't look for lost pets."

"But you don't understand. She's a very smart dinosaur. Why, it's almost as if she was human. She can practically talk."

"In that case," said Officer Tran, "you'd better hang up. She could be trying to call home right now."

A man came into a store riding a dinosaur. The storekeeper looked up and whistled. "Hey, that's pretty impressive. Where did you get it?"

"New Jersey," said the dinosaur.

Two Tyrannosaurus broke into a cookie factory and ate everything in sight. When they were done, the first one's stomach made an awful noise.

"Maybe you ate too much," said the second Tyrannosaurus.

"Naw," said the other. "That's just the way the cookie rumbles."

Mr. Fuddy opened up his refrigerator and found a Gravitholus inside.

"What are you doing here," Mr. Fuddy exclaimed.

"Isn't this a Westinghouse?" the Gravitholus asked.

"Well, yes," Mr. Fuddy stammered.

"Then I'm westing," said the dinosaur.

Philip loved dinosaurs. In fact, he loved them so much that he had a statue of one made and put in his front yard. One morning he looked out the window and saw that it had been painted in green and yellow stripes.

He ran outside and saw two cans of green and yellow paint sitting in front of his new neighbor's garage. He went over and pounded on the front door. "Hey!" he yelled. "Did you paint stripes on my dinosaur?"

The door opened and there stood a man who was so big that he made the Incredible Hulk look like a 98-pound weakling. "Yeah, I did," the bodybuilder replied.

Philip laughed nervously. "Well, I just wanted to let you know that it's dry."

One day when Tim came to the bus stop, there was a big bite mark on the cover of his notebook.

"Boy, what happened now?" Lynne asked.

"My dinosaur was still hungry after dinner last night, so he decided to eat my notebook."

"I see you stopped him," Lynne said.

"Yeah," said Tim. "I took the words right out of his mouth."

Gina took her pet dinosaur with her everywhere. One day she went to the mall, but the security guard stopped her. "Sorry, no animals allowed in the mall."

So Gina went home and got a white cane and some sunglasses and pretended she was blind. When she got back to the mall, the security guard stopped her again. "Sorry, miss, no animals."

"But this is my seeing-eye dog," Gina said.

"That's a dinosaur. It's no seeing-eye dog."

Gina didn't miss a blink. "How should I know?"

Mr. Ryan was a big-time movie director. He was holding auditions for his next musical when a man walked in leading a baby dinosaur. "This is the greatest dinosaur singer ever born," said the man.

"Okay," Mr. Ryan said. "Show me."

The dinosaur launched in to *The Star Spangled Banner*. As soon as she finished, the door burst open and a bigger dinosaur stomped in, picked up the baby, and stomped back out.

"That was fantastic!" Mr. Ryan shouted. "But who took that kid away?"

"That was her mother. She wants her to be a lawyer."

The writer sent his agent a manuscript for a new joke book. A few weeks went by and he hadn't heard anything, so he called his agent.

"There's good news and there's bad news," the agent said.

"Okay, what's the good news?"

"Ballantine ate it up," she replied.

"So what's the bad news?" the writer asked.

"Ballantine is my dinosaur."

"My dinosaur is very smart," Pam told Lori.

"I don't believe you," Lori said.

"Come on." And they walked into the backyard, where the dinosaur was. "How much is seven times zero?"

The dinosaur was silent.

"See," said Lori. "It isn't smart at all."

"Hey," said Pam. "It said *nothing*, didn't it?"

David went into the candy store, but there was no one behind the counter. He rang the little bell, but no one came. "Hey," he shouted. "How about some service!"

A Stegosaurus came out from the back. "Gee whiz, can't a guy even unpack some gum around here? What's your hurry, sonny?" it said.

David just stared at him.

"Listen, I'm talking to you. Do you want some candy or not?" the Stegosaurus said.

David still stared at him.

The Stegosaurus leaned over the counter. "I said, do you want some candy or not?"

"Sure," said David. "But what happened to the nice old Triceratops who used to work here?"

Darren had always wanted a little brother. One day his father told him that he was going to get his wish. His mother got bigger and bigger, until finally she went to the hospital and gave birth to a little boy.

Darren's father took him to see his mother and his new brother. Darren watched with wide eyes the whole time.

In the car on the way back home, Darren's father said, "See, son, isn't the miracle of birth wonderful?"

"It sure is, dad. But next time, do you think Mom could make me a dinosaur?"

Gus the Goofasaurus was walking through the jungle when he came to a tunnel through a hill. He tried to walk into it, but he was too tall. So he picked up a rock and started smashing away at the top of the tunnel to make it bigger.

Along came Susie the Smartasaurus. "What are you doing?" she cried. Gus told her.

"Silly," she said. "You don't have to work so hard. Just dig out the floor of the tunnel so it's lower."

"That shows how much you know," said Gus. "It isn't my legs that are too long, it's my head that won't fit."

"It's a beautiful day, don't you think?" said one Brontosaurus.

"Oh sure, it's great," snarled another. "I got chased by a Tyrannosaurus, I got stuck in the mud at the lake, and I have an upset stomach from eating poison oak. It couldn't be better."

"Well," sniffed the first, "you don't have to be saurcastic."

The two explorers came across a giant cave. The walls were decorated with drawings of Pterodactyl and Triceratops. Down the middle were a row of stone boxes. They spent hours pushing the lid off of one. Inside was the perfectly preserved skeleton of a Scleromochlus.

"What an incredible find," said Livingstone. "This is an ancient reptile burial site. We'll be famous."

"Yeah," said Stonely. "But what exactly are these boxes?"

"You idiot, those are the saurcophaguses."

Linda went to work mowing Mr. Crank's lawn. "I'm very particular about how my lawn is mowed," he told her. "You have to mow from left to right. If you don't, I will get very angry. And if I get really angry, I turn into a Tyrannosaurus."

Linda thought he was joking, so she started mowing the lawn from right to left. Mr. Crank came stomping out of his house.

"Darn it," he yelled. "That's not how I told you to do it. I'm warning you. Don't make me angry."

Linda started mowing the lawn the way he wanted, but pretty soon she forgot all about what Mr. Crank had said, and she started going the wrong way.

He came running out again. "Blast it," he screamed. "Do it the way I told you, or I won't be responsible for the consequences."

Well, sure enough, five minutes later Linda was mowing the lawn the wrong way again. Mr. Crank came out the door, but by the time he reached the edge of the porch his skin had turned to leather. He took another two steps and he had big sharp teeth. After another step he'd grown to be fifteen feet tall.

Linda took off running. A block away she turned around and Mr. Crank was still following her. "Geez," she shouted, "you don't have to get saur about it."

Hank was in the Navy for about two months when his mother wrote him that his pet Brontosaurus was sick and that he'd better come home. He went to his captain and asked permission.

"I'm sorry, son, but I can't let you go. How would I explain it to the admiral?"

"That's easy," said Hank. "Tell him you gave me saur leave."

Two cavemen were taking a long path through the jungle. They came around a bend, and there was a smaller path leading away from the one they were on. It went straight in the direction they needed to go, while the main path wandered off in another direction.

"Let's go this way," said the first.

"Oh, no," said the second. "It's dangerous. We might get eaten alive down there. It's full of monsters."

"Why?"

"Because it's the saur-cut."

A dinosaur walked into the fancy restaurant and sat down at a table. A waiter came over to take its order.

"I'll have the frog legs in the Cajun barbecue sauce, very rare, with a side order of chicken fried rice."

"Very good, sir," said the waiter.

"Excuse me," said a man at the next table. "But don't you think this is a little strange?"

"Not at all, sir," the waiter replied. "That's what he orders every week."

Mr. Cooper was doing a brisk business in selling Barney the Dinosaur toys. But because his shop was crowded, he had to keep them on a high shelf behind the cash register. One day a little girl came in and asked for a Barney toy. Mr. Cooper got the ladder out, climbed up, got the toy, got down and sold it to the little girl.

No sooner had he put the ladder back than another little girl came in. "I would like a Barney toy, please," she said. So Mr. Cooper dragged the ladder back out, climbed up again, and got the toy. Just as he was about to start back down the ladder, a third little girl came in.

"I suppose you want one of these Barney toys, too," he said.

"No, sir," she replied.

So Mr. Cooper came down the ladder, sold Barney to the second little girl, then put the ladder away. "Now then," he said to the third little girl, "what can I help you with?"

She smiled. "I'd like *two* Barney toys, please."

Gus the Goofasaurus stubbed his toe, so he went to Dino Village to see the doctor. He walked into an office and put his foot up on the counter. "Doc, you gotta help me. There's something wrong with my toe."

The dinosaur behind the counter looked at his toe for a moment and said, "Seems fine to me. It's your eyes that I'd be worried about?"

"Why?"

"Because the sign out front says *hardware*."

Larry wanted to work at Jurassic Village. The only job they had was in the circus. The manager took him to the tent and pointed to the center ring. A beautiful woman walked into a cage of dinosaurs. She stood stock still as ten Tyrannosaurus Rex walked up to her, licked her all over, and walked away.

The manager turned to Larry. "Think you can do that?"

"Sure," said Larry. "But get those dinosaurs out of there first."

A Scotsman was visiting Alaska. As he pulled into a restaurant alongside the road, he saw a moose in the parking lot.

"Pardon me," he asked the waitress inside. "What would that animal outside be?"

The waitress looked out. "Oh, that. That's a moose."

"A moose!" exclaimed the Scotsman. "If that's your moose, then your cats must be as big as dinosaurs."

A dinosaur rushed into the veterinarian's office with a toothache. In nothing flat the vet had the tooth out and the pain was gone.

"Thank you, Doc," the Stegosaurus said. "I can't pay you, but I'll be back with your reward."

About twenty minutes later the dinosaur returned with a live lobster.

"Why, thank you," said the vet. "I guess I'll take him home for dinner."

"I wouldn't do that," the Stegosaurus replied. "He's already had dinner. But I know he'd like to see a movie."

A Triceratops went into a soda fountain and ordered a chocolate malted. He drank most of it, but as soon as he drained the glass he spit the last couple of ounces at the man behind the counter.

"Oh, I'm so sorry," the Triceratops said. "I can't help myself. It's a nervous habit I have. I'm so ashamed of myself."

"Well, you'd better get some help," said the counterman. "See a psychiatrist."

"I will," promised the dinosaur.

A few weeks went by and the dinosaur came back into the soda fountain. He ordered another chocolate malted, and, sure enough, he spit the last of it out all over the counterman.

"Hey," the counterman shouted. "I thought you were going to get some therapy for that."

"I *did*," said the Triceratops proudly. "And now I'm not ashamed anymore."

A guy walked into a bar in New York City with a Camptosaurus on a leash. He sat down on a stool, and as luck would have it, the guy next to him was a talent agent.

"Listen," the man said. "You gotta see Cam here do his act. He's fantastic. Hit it, Cam."

All of a sudden the dinosaur starts singing like Frank Sinatra.

The guy yells out, "Joan Rivers," and the Camptosaur starts telling really funny jokes.

Then the guy says "George Burns," and the dinosaur whips out a cigar and starts telling even funnier jokes.

"Well," the guy asks, "what do you think of Cam?"

The agent pulls the dinosaur aside and says, "Listen, pal, forty years I been in this business already. I know from talent. Let me tell you something ... just be yourself."

In the same bar a week later a woman walked in with a baby Diplodocus on a leash. She sat down at the bar and ordered a drink for herself and a bucket of ginger ale for her dinosaur.

As soon as it finished drinking its ginger ale, the dinosaur reared up on its hind legs and started singing songs from *Guys and Dolls*.

"That's incredible," said the bartender. "How much do you want for the dinosaur?"

"Buy me another round on the house and he's yours," the woman said.

"Done," and the bartender gave them each a fresh drink. "But I don't understand why you're selling him so cheap."

"Heck," the woman said. "The only show he knows is *Guys and Dolls*."

Two Tyrannosaurus were watching television, and *Godzilla* came on. They watched for a while, and then one turned to the other. "That dinosaur is a terrible actor. His movements aren't natural, and he sounds like he swallowed a horn from a Honda."

"Dummy," said its friend. "That isn't a real dinosaur. It's a fake."

"Really?" said the first Tyrannosaurus. "You'd never know."

Ook and Mook were two cavemen who lived in the same cave. The day dinosaur season started, they made a hundred clam bet about who would catch the first dinosaur. Pretty soon they started to argue about it, and Ook jumped up, grabbed his spear, and ran out of the cave and into the jungle.

Mook just sat there for about an hour. All of a sudden a Tyrannosaurus Rex stuck its head into the cave. "You know a guy named Ook?" it asked.

Mook was trembling so hard he could barely nod his head.

"Well, he owes you a hundred clams."

A real rough looking guy walks into a restaurant in Canada, followed by a Tyrannosaurus Rex. All the customers run out the door.

"Do you serve Americans here?" he yells.

"Sure," says the waitress. "We serve anyone."

"Good," the man growled. "I'll have a hamburger, and my dinosaur here will have an American."

A man walks into a bar in the Bronx, followed by his pet dinosaur. The TV is showing the Yankees game, and everybody is watching, including the dinosaur. Finally, in the sixth inning, the Yankees score a run. The dinosaur goes crazy, jumping up and down, shaking the bar.

"Boy," says the bartender. "Your dinosaur sure likes the Yankees. What does he do when they win a game?"

"I don't know," the man says. "I've only had him eight years."

Jack and Jill sat down to watch *The Wizard of Oz* on television. Jill's pet dinosaur Rocky was in the room and his eyes were glued to the set. He cried when Miss Gulch tried to take Toto away, he laughed at the Scarecrow, and he cheered when Dorothy threw water on the Wicked Witch.

"Golly," said Jack. "I can't believe the way Rocky reacted to the movie."

"Me neither," said Jill. "He *hated* the book."

Ronald, George, and Dan needed a fourth person for their golf team. Dan said his new next door neighbor had some clubs; maybe he could be persuaded to play. The only problem was that his neighbor was a dinosaur.

"Okay by me," Ronald said, and George agreed to go along too.

The next day they met Dan and his neighbor—a great big Tyrannosaurus Rex—at the golf course. The dinosaur stepped up to the first tee and swung, and the ball sailed five hundred yards to the putting green. It came down an inch from the hole.

"That's all I need to see," said Ronald, and George agreed.

So Rex became the fourth member of the team. The big tournament was the following Saturday. Ronald, George, and Dan were all smiles as Rex stepped up to tee and hit another beautiful ball five hundred yards. The others teed off as well, and all four of them trotted down to the green.

Rex's ball was about six inches from the hole. The caddie handed him a putter, Rex swung . . . and hit the ball five hundred yards.

Two scientists were excavating a very promising dig. Finally, after three years of work, they uncovered the bones of the largest Goofasaurus they had ever seen. But buried right next to the bones was a car door.

"What do you suppose *this* is doing here?" said the first scientist.

"Well, in the Cretaceous period all the land about us was a great desert," said the other.

"So?"

"Dummy. If it got hot while it was traveling, the Goofasaurus wanted to be able to roll a window down."

A Tyrannosaurus came into the restaurant and sat down at a table. "Hey," he growled at the waiter, "it's too hot in here. Turn up the air conditioning."

"Certainly," said the waiter.

When the waiter came to take his order, the Tyrannosaurus said, "Can't you do anything right? Now it's too cold. Turn that air conditioning off!"

"Right away," said the waiter.

As soon as the waiter brought the Tyrannosaurus's food, the dinosaur bellowed, "*Now* it's too hot in here again! Turn the air conditioning back on!"

"As you wish," said the waiter.

As the waiter walked back to the kitchen, a Brontosaurus at another table waved him over. "Isn't that Tyrannosaurus driving you crazy?" she asked.

"No, ma'am," the waiter said quietly. "I'm driving him crazy. We don't have an air conditioner."

All her life, Tina the Triceratops had been terrorized by Tom the Tyrannosaurus. The only way Tina could get to the local watering hole was to walk by the cave where Tom lived, and every day he would chase her.

Finally, Tina was creeping along the jungle path, trying to pass Tom's cave without attracting any attention. When she got to Tom's cave she noticed that another Tyrannosaurus was sitting outside, weeping. The dinosaur was crying so hard that Tina walked over and asked, "What's the matter?"

"It's my husband, Tom, he's dead," the Tyrannosaurus sobbed.

"Oh, excuse me," said Tina. "I'll be moving along."

But a few minutes later she was back.

"I'm sorry," she apologized, "but what did you say was the matter?"

"Tom is dead!" wailed the widow.

"Sorry to trouble you," Tina said.

Not five minutes went by before she was back again. "What happened to Tom?" she asked.

"He's dead!" the Tyrannosaurus screamed. "Can't you get that through your thick head? Why do you keep asking me?"

"Well," said Tina, "it just sounds so good to hear you say it."

Gus the Goofasaurus announced that he was moving from California to Canada.

"Why leave all this beautiful sunshine behind?" asked his friend.

"Because, if you live in Canada and it gets cold, you can always come back to California. But if you live in California and it gets cold, where can you go?"

A caveman was captured by a Tyrannosaurus.

"Any last words?" the Tyrannosaurus said.

"You can talk!" the caveman exclaimed.

"Yes," said the Tyrannosaurus. "I was found as a baby by a group of nomadic hunters, and they raised me and taught me to speak."

"But you still eat people?"

"Sure," said the Tyrannosaurus. "But now I use a knife and fork."

Gus the Goofasaurus ran into the train station.

"Quick," he said. "How fast can I get to Seattle?"

The stationmaster said, "the train outside goes to Seattle in ten minutes."

"Great," said Gus. "That's fast."

For his birthday, Gus got a jigsaw puzzle. The next year he got another one.

"Gee," said Gus, "I'm not finished with the first one yet."

"Not finished?" said his friend. "Why are you taking so long?"

"I've only taken twelve months. And on the side of the box it says 'three to five years.'"

One Tuesday Eunice's mother brought her boss home for dinner.

Eunice came into the dining room just as everyone sat down. She had a puzzled look on her face.

"Excuse me," she said to the guest. "Are you Mommy's new boss?"

"No, dear," the man replied. "I've worked for the company for forty years."

"Oh," said Eunice, "I'm confused."

"Why," said the boss.

"Because, Mommy said that tonight she was bringing that old dinosaur she works for home for dinner."

A Navy submarine ran aground on an island in the South Pacific. The captain ordered the periscope raised and looked around.

"Great Scott!" he cried. "There are dinosaurs out there."

"Let me see," said the first mate. "You're right, sir. They're gathered all around the sub. They seem to be talking to one another."

"Send for Morris," said the Captain. "He reads lips and speaks ten languages. Maybe he can understand what they're saying."

Morris came and looked out of the periscope. "Well, sir," he announced, "I've got good news and bad news."

"What's the good news?" the Captain asked.

"I can understand what they're saying."

"What's the bad news?"

"They're waiting for somebody to come back with a can opener."

Arnold and Elaine went to a big house for a party. On the wall was a stuffed Tyrannosaurus head.

"Wow," said Arnold. "Look at that."

"Yeah," said Elaine. "He must have been running awfully fast when he hit that wall."

The absent-minded dinosaur was walking down the hill when she tripped. She started rolling and hit three trees, six birds, and a chicken.

When she got to the bottom she picked herself up and said, "Who made all that noise?"

Three dinosaurs were walking through the forest. A terrible storm came up, and the thunder was so loud that they could barely hear each other.

"Windy, isn't it?" said the first one.

"No," shouted the second. "It's Thursday."

"Me, too," yelled the third. "Let's get something to drink."

Gus the Goofasaurus and his mother had to make a trip across the Himalayas. His mother gave him some gum. "This will help keep your ears from popping when we reach high altitudes."

They made the long trip and finally reached a lower elevation.

"Are you tired?" Gus's mother asked.

"What?" said Gus.

"Are you tired?" his mother said more loudly.

"No," said Gus. "But I can hardly hear you. How do I get this gum out of my ears?"

The great auction house was selling off a collection of rare dinosaur fossils.

"What am I offered for this handsome Dryosaurus skull?" cried the auctioneer.

"Idiot!" called a scientist in the third row. "That's the skull of an Enigmasaurus."

The auctioneer smiled. "Well, folks, that just shows how little I know about the Bible."

Elaine was applying for a job as an assistant to the well-known dinosaur authority, Dr. Alice Saurus. The third question on the application was "What is the significance of the word 'sauropod?'

Elaine wrote, "It means that I won't get this job."

Walter Crankcase was a famous journalist. He had travelled deep into Africa to find the last surviving Tyrannosaurus Rex and interview her.

"It must be pretty lonely being the last Tyrannosaurus," Crankcase said. "How can you stand it?"

"Oh, it's not so bad," the dinosaur replied. "I keep pretty busy, and every day I have someone over for dinner."

Norman had found a perfectly preserved Diplodocus skull in his backyard when he was digging his new swimming pool. Excited, he called the Natural History Museum.

"I need to speak to someone about selling a dinosaur skull," he told the museum operator.

"Just a moment, sir," the operator replied. "I'll connect you with our head buyer."

Never Cross a Dinosaur with a Skunk

Why do mining companies and bridge-building companies hire a lot of dinosaurs?
Because they are experts with dino-mite!

What time of day are dinosaurs usually born?
Anytime they want!

How much tender, loving care do baby dinosaurs need?
A lot!

BABY DINOSAUR: "What time is it?"
MOTHER DINOSAUR: "Why?"
BABY DINOSAUR: "What difference does it make?"
MOTHER DINOSAUR: "None."
BABY DINOSAUR: "So, what time is it?"
MOTHER DINOSAUR: "The same time it was when it didn't make any difference!"

"Hey, Mom, this is the worst dinosaur steak I ever tasted!"
"I'm not surprised, since it comes from a cow!"

"Hello, police department? I've lost my dinosaur and . . ."
"Sorry, this is not a job for the police."
"You don't understand, this is a very intelligent dinosaur."
"In that case, don't worry. If she's that smart, she'll find her way home!"

"Did you hear about dial-a-dino?"
"No."
"It's a new dating service for dinosaurs."

"Did you hear about the problem on the train that was transporting four hundred dinosaurs to a new zoo in Canada?"
"No. What was the problem?"
"They couldn't all eat at the same time in the dino-car!"

What do you do when you catch a real dinosaur?
Scream for help!

"I once wanted to become a dinosaur, but I changed my mind."
"Why?"
"Because you never get picked for the tennis team!"

What do you get when you cross a dinosaur with a dinosaur?
A dinosaur, of course!

What simple affliction brought about the extinction of dinosaurs?
A lack of caring!

Why don't dinosaurs play tennis?
Because they don't know the rules!

Who was the most popular dinosaur actor?
Dino Martin.

What do you call it when a thousand dinosaurs get sent to the pound?
A mess!

What do you call a dinosaur who can't point?
Dino-pointing!

What do you call a dinosaur with flat feet?
An archosaurus!

What do you get when you cross a dinosaur with a crocodile?
A crocodilia!

What do you get when you cross a dinosaur with a tyrant?
A tyrannosaurus!

Why do dinosaurs sing in forests?
That's show business!

How do you stop a 2000-pound dinosaur from charging?
Take away its credit cards!

How do you catch a runaway dinosaur?
Hide behind a tree and pray!

How does a dinosaur from Georgia greet another dinosaur?
With southern dino-pitality!

Can a dinosaur really be worth thousands of dollars?
Yes, if it saves all its money!

What is a dinosaur's favorite composer?
B[r]ach-iosaurus!

Who is the host for Masterpiece Theater?
Allosaurus Cooke!

What is the favorite musical in dinosaur-land?
My Fair Dino!

What do you get when you cross a dinosaur with a hyena?
A dinosaur with a very funny laugh!

What do you do with a sick dinosaur?
Give it two aspirins and chicken soup!

When can you take your dinosaur to a dance?
Whenever it wants!

Can anything be smarter than a dinosaur that can count?
Yes, a spelling bee!

Where do you find toy dinosaurs?
In a toy store, of course!

"Help, Doctor, my dinosaur swallowed my pen."
"I'll be right there, but what are you doing in the meantime?"
"Using a pencil!"

Why don't dinosaurs go to the dentist?
It's too expensive!

DINOSAUR: "What's a fly doing in my soup?"
WAITER: "The backstroke!"

What is the most stressful thing that mother dinosaurs are forced to deal with?
Finding sneakers that fit their babies!

Did you hear about the 5000-foot dinosaur?
Don't try and kid me. I know dinosaurs have only four feet!

DINOSAUR ONE: "Are you superstitious?"
DINOSAUR TWO: "No."
DINOSAUR ONE: "Then lend me thirteen dollars, please!"

DINOSAUR ONE: "Do you write with your left hand or your right hand?"
DINOSAUR TWO: "My left hand."
DINOSAUR ONE: "That's funny. I usually write with a fountain pen!"

DINOSAUR ONE: "Do you want to play in the snow?"
DINOSAUR TWO: "Yes. Do you have a sled?"
DINOSAUR ONE: "Yes. We can share it."
DINOSAUR TWO: "OK. I'll have it for downhill, and you can have it for uphill!"

CHILD DINOSAUR: "Mommy, the teacher yelled at me today."
MOTHER DINOSAUR: "Why?"
CHILD DINOSAUR: "For something I didn't do."
MOTHER DINOSAUR: "What?"
CHILD DINOSAUR: "My homework!"

DINOSAUR ONE: "Have you met the dinosaur that emigrated here from Canada?"
DINOSAUR TWO: "No. What's her name?"
DINOSAUR ONE: "Albertasaurus!"

Why do dinosaurs sleep a lot?
Because they're tired!

Why don't dinosaurs like to jog?
It hurts their tails!

Why don't dinosaurs like to play baseball?
It's very difficult to find baseball caps that fit!

Do dinosaurs make good pets?
No.
Why not?
They take up too much room in the bed!

Did you hear about the dinosaur who rescued the bus from a ravine?
He was a real dino-mo!

Do brother and sister dinosaurs fight?
Of course. They're no different from brother and sister elephants!

Did you hear about the dinosaur that drank too much wine?
It became a famous opera singer!

Did you hear about the dinosaur that dove into Lake Tahoe?
It was permanently transformed into Tahoe Canyon!

Why did the dinosaur go to sleep with her glasses on?
It wanted to focus on its dreams!

Why did the dinosaur put a candy bar under its pillow?
It wanted to make sure it had sweet dreams!

Do you know how to train a dinosaur?
Very carefully!

Why was the baby dinosaur being punished?
Because it wouldn't eat its brussels sprouts!

Why does everyone call that animal a giraffe?
Because it's not a dinosaur!

What is a dinosaur's favorite day of the week?
Dino-day!

Did you hear about the Ceratosaurus that married the Barosaurus?
No. What happened?
I don't know. They're still trying to figure it out!

What do you do when a dinosaur makes a mistake?
Ignore it!

What do you call a dinosaur who eats too much?
A Gorgosaur!

What do you get when you cross a dinosaur with a wild dog?
A dino-go!

What do you get when you cross a dinosaur with a soprano?
A diva-dino!

What do dinosaurs like to play with instead of building blocks?
People!

Why wasn't the dinosaur successful?
It didn't believe in itself!

What do you get when you cross a dinosaur and a tenor?
Something even stranger than a tenor!

Who writes books about dinosaurs?
I don't know, but I'm sure it isn't a ghostwriter!

What did one dinosaur say to the other dinosaur?
"Do you really believe in people?"

What do you get when you cross a dinosaur with a piece of gum?
A Yangchuanosaurus!

How far can a dinosaur walk into a forest?
Only halfway ... then it's walking out!

In what language should you write to a dinosaur living in France?
French, silly!

How do you teach a dinosaur to dance?
With music and a lot of patience!

What is the room a dinosaur doesn't need?
A small one!

What guests did the dinosaur invite to its party?
Anyone it could dig up!

What do you get from a two-headed dinosaur?
Double talk!

What happened to the dinosaur that swallowed laundry detergent?
It stayed clean forever!

What should every elegant dinosaur wear?
Dino-monds, of course!

What do you call a dinosaur on skid row?
A dino-wino!

What do you call a dinosaur on a tricycle?
Strange!

What do you call a dozen dinosaurs?
A bunch!

If a dinosaur was after you, what kind of steps would you take?
Big ones!

What do dinosaurs in a nursery like to hear?
Dino-rhymes!

What do you get if you cross a dinosaur with a vampire?
A dinosaur that lives forever!

What do you get when you cross a dinosaur with a cow?
A Carnosaurus!

What do you call a dinosaur who lives in Brazil?
A Riojasaurus!

What happened to the dinosaur that swallowed a bird?
Absolutely nothing!

What happened when the girl Tyrannosaurus met the boy Tyrannosaurus?
It was love at first bite!

Why did the dinosaur eat the tightrope walker?
It wanted a well-balanced diet!

What do you call a dinosaur that gazes at the moon?
A romantic!

What is forty feet tall and makes a click-click noise?
A ballpoint dinosaur!

What do you get if you cross a dinosaur with a kangaroo?
Bouncy thumps!

BABY DINOSAUR: "Mommy, I hate my friend's guts."
MOTHER DINOSAUR: "Then leave them on the side of your plate and finish your lunch!

What does a dinosaur have for dinner?
A lot!

What do you call a dinosaur who eats crackers in bed?
Annoying!

What do you call a dinosaur's favorite car?
A dino-Taurus!

What did the dinosaur say when she stepped on the campfire?
"Ouch!"

What does a dinosaur call his parents?
Mommy and Daddy!

PERSON ONE: "Did you hear about the dinosaur that can't eat candy?"
PERSON TWO: "No. What's the problem?"
PERSON ONE: "He has dinobetes!"

What do dinosaurs cook when they're in a hurry?
Fast people!

What do you get when you cross a dinosaur with a pickle?
A sour-saur!

What do you get when you cross a dinosaur with a photocopy machine?
A dino-copy!

What do you have when your dinosaur
falls in the bathtub?
A wet pet!

Who is a dinosaur's favorite actor?
Charles Brontosaurus.

Why did the dinosaur cross the road?
To get to McDonald's.

Why did the dinosaur buy a sweater?
Because it didn't know how to knit!

What do you call a dinosaur without teeth?
A vegetarian!

How do you make a dinosaur laugh?
Carefully!

How do you make a dinosaur stew?
Keep it waiting for hours!

How can you tell when there is a dinosaur
in your refrigerator?
Its footprints are in the cheesecake!

What is green and has four legs, a long
tail, and a trunk?
A seasick dinosaur on vacation!

How many dinosaurs does it take to change a light bulb?
Four—one to hold the bulb and three to turn the room!

How can you tell the difference between a dinosaur and a cat?
If this is difficult for you, you're in trouble!

What do you get if you cross a dinosaur with a gorilla?
Who knows, but getting a seat on the train wouldn't be a problem!

What do you get if you cross a dinosaur with a ventriloquist?
A dinosaur that talks to itself.

What kind of dinosaurs go to psychiatrists?
Insecure ones!

What do you get when you cross a dinosaur with a computer?
A thousand-pound know-it-all!

What happened to the dinosaur that covered himself with vanishing cream?
Nobody knows!

What do you call a dinosaur with one eye?
A dino-clops!

What do you get when you cross a dinosaur with a penguin?
A dinosaur ready for a formal party!

When is a dinosaur not a dinosaur?
When it's a dear!

What do you call a dinosaur that likes bagels with cream cheese and lox?
Smart!

What do you get when you cross a dinosaur with an octopus?
A dinosaur that needs four pairs of running shoes!

What do you get when you cross a dinosaur with a lion?
A dinosaur that needs a haircut!

Why did the dinosaur take a bath?
To get clean!

What do you give a dinosaur with a cough?
Dinotussin!

Why did the dinosaur go out with a prune?
Because he couldn't get a date!

Why don't dinosaurs like to swim in pools?
The chlorine hurts their eyes!

What do you get if a dinosaur steps on your foot?
A soreasaurus!

What did one dinosaur say to another dinosaur?
"Hello!"

What do you call a dinosaur with a white beard, a red hat, and a team of reindeer?
Dino Claus!

What do you do to a dinosaur that cheats at cards?
Nothing!

What do you get when you cross a dinosaur with a porcupine?
A Pricklysaurus!

What do you call an aerobics class with dinosaurs?
Dino-cize!

What do you get when you cross a dinosaur with a turtle?
A Snaposaurus!

What do you get when you cross a dinosaur with a woodpecker?
A dinosaur proficient at Morse code!

What kind of dinosaur works at the United Nations?
A diplo-dino!

Why should dinosaurs drink decaffeinated coffee?
There's nothing worse than a nervous dinosaur!

What do dinosaurs wear?
Clothes, what else!

What do you get when you cross a dinosaur with a fish?
A dinosaur that has an aversion to nets!

What do you get when you cross a galaxy with a dinosaur?
A dinosaur with his head in the clouds!

If you saw forty-nine dinosaurs walking down the street with shoes and one walking without shoes, what would this prove?
One out of fifty dinosaurs doesn't wear shoes!

When is it dangerous to play with dinosaurs in the jungle?
Anytime!

What do you get when you cross a stage-struck dinosaur with a pig?
A big ham!

How much does a psychiatrist charge a dinosaur?
$100 for the visit and $1000 for the broken furniture!

How do you keep a dinosaur from going down the drain?
Tie a rock to its tail!

What do you get when you cross a dinosaur with an electric eel?
A lot of volts!

How do you make a dinosaur laugh?
Tell it an elephant joke!

What do you do if you find a dinosaur in your bed?
Sleep somewhere else!

What do you call a dinosaur with earplugs?
Since it can't hear you, it doesn't matter!

How mad can a dinosaur get?
Very!

What does a dinosaur do when it loses its temper?
Believe me, you don't want to know!

What do you call a dinosaur that moans a lot?
A Groanosaurus!

What do you say to an Italian dinosaur in the morning?
"Buon giorno!"

What do you get when you cross a dinosaur with a refrigerator?
Large ice cubes!

What do you get when you cross a dinosaur with a homing pigeon?
A dinosaur that never gets lost!

What did the dinosaur say when it took off its clothes?
Nothing. A dinosaur doesn't wear clothes!

What do you get when you cross a dinosaur with a racing car?
A dinosaur who is raring to go!

What do you get when you cross a Nanotyrannus with electricity?
An energized dinosaur!

What do you get when you cross a dinosaur with a parrot?
A dinosaur that talks too much!

What do you get when you cross a dinosaur with a fish?
A Slimosaurus!

What do you get if you cross a dinosaur with a parakeet?
A messy cage!

What do you get when you cross a Diplodocus with a skunk?
A strong odor!

How do dinosaurs learn to play the violin?
Carefully!

What do you get when you cross a dinosaur with an oyster?
A very large pearl!

What should you do if you meet a dinosaur?
Smile!

What do you call a 5,000-pound female dinosaur?
"Ms.!"

Why did the teacher excuse the dinosaur?
Because she's smart!

What do you get if you cross a Barosaurus with a snail?
A very slow dinosaur!

What do you get when you cross a dinosaur with Dracula?
A big problem!

Why did the dinosaur jump over the moon?
No particular reason!

What do you call a dinosaur that drinks too much?
A Drunkosaurus!

What do you get when you cross a dinosaur with a locomotive?
A dinosaur that follows the right track!

What is large, powerful, prehistoric, and costs six million dollars?
A bionic dinosaur!

What do you get when you cross a Ceratosaurus with a witch?
A dinosaur that needs a large broom!

What do you call a dinosaur that lives "over the rainbow?"
A Munchkinsaurus!

What do you get when you cross a dinosaur with a rat?
An animal that craves plenty of cheese!

What do you get when you cross a dinosaur with peanut butter?
A sticky mess!

What do you get when you cross a dinosaur with an ocean?
Tidal waves!

What do political dinosaurs do when they are too old to run for public office?
They take limousines!

Who was a favorite politician in 1993?
Bill Clintonsaurus!

What do you do with a hyperopic [farsighted] dinosaur?
Buy it reading glasses!

What do you get when you cross a dinosaur with a sheep and a kangaroo?
Very old and large woolen jumpers!

What do you get when you cross a dinosaur with a television?
A big screen!

What do you get when you cross a dinosaur with a tissue?
The Big Sneeze!

If a Tyrannosaurus traveled into space, what would it be called?
A dino-naut!

What do young dinosaurs argue about when traveling by car to visit Grandma?
Who gets to sit by the window!

What do you get when you cross a dinosaur with a pig?
An Oinkasaurus!

What do you get when you cross a dinosaur with a minister?
Well-attended sermons!

What do you call a dinosaur that eats potato chips daily?
The Big Dipper!

What do you get when you cross a dinosaur with a weeping willow?
A very sad beast!

What do dinosaurs eat?
Food!

What do Pterodactyl celebrate every two hundred years?
Their Dino-tennial!

What did the waiter say to the dinosaur that complained about holes in his cheese?
"Just eat the cheese and leave the holes on your plate!"

What do you get when you cross an Ultrasaurus with a beagle?
A dinosaur with funny ears!

What do you get when you cross a Jurassic Steneosaurus with a grape?
Who cares?

What do you get when you cross a dinosaur with a cabbage?
An animal people tend to "leaf" behind!

What would you get if you threw a Sauropod into the Pacific Ocean?
An angry, wet dinosaur!

What animal looks most like a dinosaur?
Another dinosaur!

How do dinosaurs contact each other?
By telephone!

DINOSAUR ONE: "When I was young, I was told that if I made ugly faces, my face would stay that way."
DINOSAUR TWO: "You can't say that you weren't warned!"

How do you tell the difference between a girl dinosaur and a boy dinosaur?
Ask your mother or father!

FATHER DINOSAUR: "Don't you think our son gets all his brains from me?"
MOTHER DINOSAUR: "Probably. I still have all of mine!"

NEIGHBOR: "Does your baby brother talk yet?"
YOUNG DINOSAUR: "No. He doesn't have to. He gets everything by screaming!"

What do you call a dinosaur that designs buildings?
An Archaeopteryx!

What do you call a Pterodactyl vampire?
A Bloodasaurus!

Where do most musical dinosaurs work?
In the Brontosaurus Philharmonic!

What is a dinosaur's favorite magazine?
Triceratops Weekly!

What do you call a dinosaur that enjoys cooking?
A gastronosaurus!

What is a dinosaur's favorite ice cream?
Bronto-Daz!

What do you get when you cross an owl with an Allosaurus?
An owl that has difficulty balancing on tree branches!

How do you describe a dinosaur in love?
Troubled, like all other incurable romantics!

Why don't dinosaurs like to eat in restaurants?
It's difficult for them to keep napkins on their laps!

What do you get when you cross a dinosaur with an ocean liner?
A Titanosaur!

What is the best way to photograph a dinosaur?
With a camera!

How do you get a dinosaur to clean its room?
Forget it!

Who is a popular novelist among dinosaurs?
Louisa May Allosaurus!

Why isn't it wise to leave dinosaurs home alone?
They watch too much television!

Why do so few dinosaurs choose careers as police officers?
It hurts to pin on a badge!

Who is a famous German dinosaur composer?
Ludwig von Brontosaurus!

ANNOUNCEMENT: The monthly dinosaur meeting has been canceled. It conflicts with the two-hour Flintstones special!

Nothing annoys a dinosaur more than aggressive people!

MOTHER DINOSAUR: "Did you tell your brother that he's a stupid dinosaur?"
YOUNG DINOSAUR: "Yes."
MOTHER DINOSAUR: "Tell him you're sorry immediately!"
YOUNG DINOSAUR: "I'm sorry that you're a stupid dinosaur!"

What do you do if a dinosaur sits next to you on an aeroplane?
Offer it your dinner!

What do you do if a dinosaur wants to buy your house?
Don't quibble over details!

Where do dinosaurs buy sneakers?
Silly questions don't deserve answers!

Why don't dinosaurs eat spicy food?
They have delicate stomachs!

Why is divorce low among dinosaurs?
They tend to digest their problems easily!

Why isn't arthritis a problem in the dinosaur community?
They eat a lowfat diet!

DINOSAUR DENTIST: "The check you gave me came back!"
DINOSAUR PATIENT: "So did my toothache!"

What do you get when you cross a Pterodactyl with a sponge?
A very thirsty dinosaur!

What do you get when you cross a Barosaurus with a toll bridge?
A dinosaur that collects quarters!

What do you call a dinosaur that is a successful business person?
An entrepreneurasaurus!

What do you get when you cross a Deinonychus and a Diplodocus?
A unique dinosaur!

What do you call a dinosaur that plays the piano?
Liberacesaurus!

What do you call a dinosaur that sings and wears ornate dresses?
A Sopranosaurus!

What do you call a small dinosaur with a large ego?
A Tenorasaurus!

What should you avoid doing when trying to get a Tyrannosaurus's attention?
Playing with its tail!

What do you say to a haughty French dinosaur?
Bonjour, ma petite!

What do you do when a Triceratops hogs the bed?
Get a larger bed!

DINOSAUR: "Doctor, will I be able to play the piano after my arm heals?"
DOCTOR: "Definitely."
DINOSAUR: "That's great. I couldn't play before!"

"Did you hear the story about the dirty dinosaur?"
"No."
"It doesn't matter. It's a mess!"

CUSTOMER: "I would like a pair of dinosaur shoes."
SALESPERSON: "OK. What size is your dinosaur?"

What do you call dinosaurs that have many children?
Probably Grandma and Grandpa!

What do you call a Lagosuchus that enjoys gardening?
A Fleurasaur!

"Did you hear about that dinosaur that hadn't slept for days?"
"No."
"It only slept at night!"

Why don't dinosaurs like to stay in hotels?
The bathtubs are too small!

What do you get when you cross a dinosaur with a psychiatrist?
A therapeutic pet!

Who were a famous dinosaur dance team?
Fred Astairasaurus and Ginger Rogerodactyl!

Which hotel do dinosaurs prefer to frequent?
The Hypacrosaurus Hilton!

What do you get when you cross a Lagosuchus with a piano?
A dinosaur that knows its scales!

What do you call a dinosaur that conducts an orchestra?
A Maestrosaurus!

What do you call a dinosaur with a high IQ?
A Geniussaurus!

Why are dinosaurs extinct?
Human error!

Why do dinosaurs prefer to drive station wagons?
More tail room!

Why do dinosaurs frequent libraries?
They love joke books about people!

Why do dinosaurs find skiing a challenge?
Maneuvering two sets of skis on a ski lift isn't easy!

Why don't dinosaurs like to work in publishing?
They prefer to eat regularly!

"Did you hear about the Tyrannosaurus editor at Ballantine?"
"No."
"She received a large bonus for her successful series of Human Joke Books!"

Who is Calvin Klein's favorite dinosaur?
Marky Markasaurus!

What kind of art do dinosaurs prefer?
Works from the Jurassic and Cretaceous periods!

Name a famous dinosaur character in Sunset Boulevard.
Norma Desmatosuchus!

What do you call a dinosaur that doesn't eat meat?
A veggiepod!

Who was a famous ballet dancer in the Mesozoic era?
Nureyevasaurus!

What do you call a dinosaur with an eating problem?
An Anorexiasaurus!

What do you call a cat that climbs on the back of a Yangchuanosaurus?
Brave!

Dino-mite!

Knock-knock.
Who's there?
Dino.
Dino who?
Dino-mite!

Knock-knock.
Who's there?
Jurassic.
Jurassic who?
Jurassic man, see a doctor fast!

Knock-knock.
Who's there?
Triassic.
Triassic who?
Triassic pack of Pepsi!

Knock-knock.
Who's there?
Bronto.
Bronto who?
Bronto buster!

Knock-knock.
Who's there?
Stega.
Stega who?
Stega claim!

Knock-knock.
Who's there?
Pterydon.
Pterydon who?
Ptery, Don, and I are friends.

Knock-knock.
Who's there?
Allosaur.
Allosaur who?
Allosaur was his fist. Then I saw stars!

Knock-knock.
Who's there?
Yvonne.
Yvonne who?
Yvonne to see the dinosaurs at the museum?

Knock-knock.
Who's there?
Ivana.
Ivana who?
Ivana pet dinosaur.

Knock-knock.
Who's there?
Wendy.
Wendy who?
Wendy dinosaurs roamed the earth, it was a long time ago.

Knock-knock.
Who's there?
Alma.
Alma who?
Alma dinosaur freak!

Knock-knock.
Who's there?
Augusta.
Augusta who?
Augusta dinosaur fossil at home!

Knock-knock.
Who's there?
Jewel.
Jewel who?
Jewel never see a live dinosaur!

Knock-knock.
Who's there?
Maya.
Maya who?
Maya favorite dinosaur is the Triceratops!

Knock-knock.
Who's there?
Iris.
Iris who?
Iris I had a Stegosaurus!

Knock-knock.
Who's there?
Betty.
Betty who?
Betty ya never saw a dinosaur with green spots!

Knock-knock.
Who's there?
Tyrone.
Tyrone who?
Tyrone-asaurus Rex.

Knock-knock.
Who's there?
Shirley.
Shirley who?
Shirley you know that dinosaurs are extinct.

Knock-knock.
Who's there?
Celeste.
Celeste who?
Celeste dinosaur died millions of years ago!

Knock-knock.
Who's there?
Joan.
Joan who?
Joan't you just love the Brontosaurus!

Knock-knock.
Who's there?
Trey.
Trey who?
Trey-ceratops!

Knock-knock.
Who's there?
Ida.
Ida who?
Ida love to see a dinosaur hatch!

Knock-knock.
Who's there?
Anita.
Anita who?
Anita write a book report on dinosaurs!

Knock-knock.
Who's there?
Minnie.
Minnie who?
Minnie dinosaurs were vegetarians!

Knock-knock.
Who's there?
Imogen.
Imogen who?
Imogen, some dinosaurs were as big as houses!

Knock-knock.
Who's there?
Hugh.
Hugh who?
Hugh look like a Tyrannosaurus!

Knock-knock.
Who's there?
Alfie.
Alfie who?
Alfie my dinosaur at lunch!

Knock-knock.
Who's there?
Esau.
Esau who?
Esau a dinosaur and got scared!

Knock-knock.
Who's there?
Sherwood.
Sherwood who?
Sherwood be nice to own a dinosaur!

Knock-knock.
Who's there?
Albert.
Albert who?
Albert you five dollars you never saw a dinosaur!

Knock-knock.
Who's there?
Malcolm.
Malcolm who?
Malcolm the dinosaurs all died out?

Knock-knock.
Who's there?
Arthur.
Arthur who?
Arthur any dinosaurs in Tibet?

Knock-knock.
Who's there?
Paley.
Paley who?
Paley-ontologist!

Knock-knock.
Who's there?
Abel.
Abel who?
Abelisaurus weighed three thousand pounds!

Knock-knock.
Who's there?
Ada.
Ada who?
Adasaurus had feet like birds!

Knock-knock.
Who's there?
Alamo.
Alamo who?
Alamosaurus was almost seventy feet long!

Knock-knock.
Who's there?
Ankle.
Ankle who?
Ankylosaurus!

Knock-knock.
Who's there?
Diana.
Diana who?
Dianasaur!

Knock-knock.
Who's there?
Fangs.
Fangs who?
Fangs for telling me a dinosaur joke!

Knock-knock.
Who's there?
Hide.
Hide who?
Hide run if I saw a dinosaur.

Knock-knock.
Who's there?
Tail.
Tail who?
Tailor me a jacket from dinosaur skin.

Knock-knock.
Who's there?
Claws.
Claws who?
Claws I say so.

Knock-knock.
Who's there?
Alda.
Alda who?
Alda dinosaurs are extinct.

Knock-knock.
Who's there?
Avocado.
Avocado who?
Avocado dinosaur. Want to see it?

Knock-knock.
Who's there?
Charlotte.
Charlotte who?
Charlotte of dinosaurs at the museum.

Knock-knock.
Who's there?
Dishes.
Dishes who?
Dishes a Tyrannosaurus Rex. Open up!

Knock-knock.
Who's there?
Hewlett.
Hewlett who?
Hewlett the dinosaurs out of their pen?

Knock-knock.
Who's there?
Hertz.
Hertz who?
Hertz to be bit by a Tyrannosaurus.

Knock-knock.
Who's there?
Juicy.
Juicy who?
Juicy that dinosaur run down the street?

Knock-knock.
Who's there?
Musket.
Musket who?
Musket in, a dinosaur is chasing me!

Knock-knock.
Who's there?
Dennis.
Dennis who?
Dennis time to go to see the dinosaurs, let me know.

Knock-knock.
Who's there?
Harry.
Harry who?
Harry up and let me in. There's a Tyrannosaurus out here.

Knock-knock.
Who's there?
Esther.
Esther who?
Esther a dinosaur in the house?

Knock-knock.
Who's there?
Carmen.
Carmen who?
Carmen see the dinosaurs at the museum.

Knock-knock.
Who's there?
Emma.
Emma who?
Emma I bigger than a Fabrosaurus?

Knock-knock.
Who's there?
Dinosaur?
Dinosaur who?
Dinosaur everything!

Knock-knock.
Who's there?
Jurassic.
Jurassic who?
Jurassic a question and maybe you'll get an answer!

Knock-knock.
Who's there?
Terror.
Terror who?
Teratosaurus!

Knock-knock.
Who's there?
Plato.
Plato who?
Plateosaurus!

Knock-knock.
Who's there?
Albert.
Albert who?
Albert Gorgosaur!

Knock-knock.
Who's there?
Saurus.
Saurus who?
Saurus Leachman.

Knock-knock.
Who's there?
Ptery.
Ptery who?
Ptery Bradshaw.

Knock-knock.
Who's there?
Freighter.
Freighter who?
Freighter open the door for a dinosaur?

Knock-knock.
Who's there?
Doughnut.
Doughnut who?
Doughnut let a Tyrannosaurus catch you.

Knock-knock.
Who's there?
Alec.
Alec who?
Alec dinosaurs.

Knock-knock.
Who's there?
Jaws.
Jaws who?
Jaws truly.

Ask Me if I'm a Brontosaurus

CASSIE: Help! A Tyrannosaurus just bit me on the leg!
ALEXANDRIA: Which one?
CASSIE: How should I know? They all look alike.

Why did the Brontosaurus have such a tough time apologizing?
It took him a long time to swallow his pride.

How come the dinosaur slept like a lawyer?
First he lied on one side, and then he lied on the other.

What time did the Bagaceratops go to the dentist?
2:30.

Did you hear about the lazy dinosaur?
He was so lazy, he stayed home and let his mind wander.

The Carnosaurus came back from a vacation in France.
"Did you learn any French?" his friend asked.
"No, but I picked up a little Italian in Nice."

ALICIA: I'm so glad I'm not a Pteranodon.
BEN: Why?
ALICIA: I can't fly!

TYRANNOSAURUS 1: Want to join me in a nice fresh Triceratops?
TYRANNOSAURUS 2: I don't think we'd fit.

How do you spell Camptosaurus backwards?
C-A-M-P-T-O-S-A-U-R-U-S B-A-C-K-W-A-R-D-S.

Mrs. Grimley wanted her class to write reports all about dinosaurs, but little Karen forgot about the assignment until she got to school that day.

Karen wrote her paper in a big hurry during lunch and turned it in. It had only one word: Extinct.

What do you call a dino after it falls off a cliff?
A sore Bronto.

When the Triceratops fell in the lake, how come it didn't get its hair wet?
It was bald.

What causes more trouble than a Tyrannosaurus in a butcher shop?
Two Tyrannosaurus in a butcher shop.

Why did the Storkosaurus stand on one leg?
Because if it stood on no legs it would fall down.

What has a long neck, weighs forty tons, and lives at the North Pole?
Rudolph the red-nosed dinosaur.

BEN: Ask me if I'm a Brontosaurus.
ALICIA: Okay, are you a Brontosaurus?
BEN: Yes. Now ask me if I'm a Triceratops.
ALICIA: Are you a Triceratops?
BEN: No, stupid. I just told you I was a Brontosaurus.

How many letters are in the dinosaur alphabet?
Nineteen: T-H-E D-I-N-O-S-A-U-R A-L-P-H-A-B-E-T.

What is the best way to prevent an infection from biting dinosaurs?
Stop biting them.

What do you call dinosaurs who fly in airplanes?
Passengers.

Why did the Goofasaurus try to eat lava?
Because he was feeling cold-blooded.

How does a dinosaur get out of a shoe box?
The same way it got in.

How many giant dinosaurs were hatched in the Jurassic period?
None. They were all babies when they hatched.

What do you call a Stegosaurus with an Ultrasaurus on his back?
Squashed.

What do you call a Triceratops that carries a Brontosaurus on its back?
Tired.

What happens to an Avisaurus when it rains?
It gets wet.

What goes clomp, clomp, clomp, squish, clomp, clomp, clomp, squish?
A Barapasaurus with a wet sneaker.

What part of a dinosaur weighed the most?
Its scales.

CHRIS: I learned in school today that it took thousands of dinosaurs to make a barrel of oil.
HARVEY: Well, if they were that lazy, no wonder they're extinct.

HARVEY: Why are you crying?
CHRIS: I wanted to get a stuffed dinosaur for my sister.
HARVEY: That shouldn't be so hard.
CHRIS: Well, it was. Nobody would trade with me.

ELAINE: Did I ever tell you about the time I came face to face with a Tyrannosaurus Rex?
ARNOLD: No!
ELAINE: I just stood there, looking at his huge, razor-sharp teeth and his cruel, wicked claws.
ARNOLD: You're so brave! What happened next?
ELAINE: I moved on to the next exhibit.

Did you hear about the resort for overwrought carnivorous dinosaurs?
It's called Tyrannosaurus Rest.

What do they call the Pacific Coast chapter of carnivorous dinosaurs?
Tyrannosaurus West.

What did Julius Caesarsaurus say when he escaped his enemies across the Rubicon?
I ran, I sore, I rest.

When did Theropods have sixteen feet?
When there were four of them.

MOTHER TYRANNOSAURUS: What are you doing?
BABY TYRANNOSAURUS: I'm chasing this Oviraptor around a tree.
MOTHER: How many times have I told you not to play with your food?

ELAINE: I think I'll go to the store and buy some dinosaur seed.
ARNOLD: But there's no such thing.
ELAINE: Then how do you grow them?

PETER: If I say, "Come here, Spike," will your Stegosaurus walk over here?
MATTHEW: No.
PETER: Why not?
MATTHEW: Because her name is Daisy.

Why did the Brontosaurus have a small breakfast?
Because a little would go a long way.

What's the most famous prehistoric short story?
The Devil and Dino Webster.

Why did Gus the Goofasaurus sign up for night school?
Because he wanted to learn to read in the dark.

Why did Gus the Goofasaurus open up his watch and dump it into his sandwich?
Because he wanted ham and cheese with the works.

Why did the Tyrannosaurus eat the alarm clock?
Because he felt like killing time.

Gus the Goofasaurus got an umbrella for his birthday. The first thing he did was to cut a hole in it.
"Why did you do that?" his friend asked.
"So I can see when it stops raining."

Why did Gus go around and around in a revolving door for an hour?
Because he was looking for the doorknob.

Gus the Goofasaurus got a job as an elevator operator, but he was fired at the end of his first day.
He couldn't remember the route.

What happened when Gus broke his leg in three places?
He said, "I'm never going back there again!"

Why did Gus wear his socks inside out?
Because they had a hole on the inside.

Why did Gus take a bicycle to bed?
Because he was afraid of walking in his sleep.

Why did Gus sit down in front of the TV set with a washcloth?
Because he was going to watch a soap opera.

Why did Gus decide to live on top of the stove?
Because he wanted to be home on the range.

Why did Gus want a sea horse?
Because he wanted to play water polo.

What did one Tyrannosaurus say to the other after they caught the Triceratops for dinner?
"Heads or tails?"

RACHEL: Listen here, I ordered dinosaur stew and I don't see anything in it that looks like dinosaur meat.
WAITER: So? We have cottage cheese and there aren't any cottages in it.

Why did so few dinosaurs get married? Because in those days, they didn't have rice, so everyone threw rocks.

"Dr. Freud, you must help my husband. He thinks he's a Brontosaurus."

"Well, have him come see me right away."

"I can't. He won't leave our house. Our next door neighbor thinks he's a Tyrannosaurus Rex!"

Dr. Freud agreed to make a house call and cured the woman's poor husband.

"There," he said. "Don't you feel better?"

"Better?" cried the man. "Before you came I was the biggest, strongest guy on the block. Now I'm nobody!"

Why could dinosaurs take long baths without being interrupted?
Because nobody had invented the telephone yet.

Did you hear about the Triceratops who got a job as a light switch?
He only worked off and on.

Did you hear about the young Tyrannosaurus who started a singing career?
He called himself Boy Jaws.

What happened in the Jurassic period when someone started giving away free Tyrannosaurus repellant?
Dinosaur-rush.

What malady strikes dinosaur trainers?
Tyrannosaur-wrist.

What did the paleontologist say to the fossil he'd discovered?
"I dig you."

Sandy went to her father and said, "Dad, where would I find dinosaur fossils?"
Her father said, "Don't ask me. Your mother puts everything away in this house."

Where did the Tyrannosaurus play?
In the Rex room.

What do you use to cook a Tyrannosaurus?
A Rexipe.

What is it called when a Tyrannosaurus plays the piano?
A Rexcital.

What are you in danger of if you drive your car without a Tyrannosaurus in the backseat?
Rexless driving.

What do you get when you ask a Tyrannosaurus for advice?
A Rexomendation.

What's the geometric form with four right angles and a Tyrannosaurus inside?
A Rextangle.

Why did the Tyrannosaurus save his empty bottles?
For Rexcycling.

Where do the Tyrannosaurs in Iceland live?
In Rexjavik.

What do you call the mess that's left over after a Tyrannosaurus eats its dinner?
The Rexage.

What did one Tyrannosaurus say to the other when it saw the herd of Brontosaurs?
"Let's go over there and Rex some havoc."

The two deputies arrived at the scene of the auto accident. The vehicle was completely mangled, there was no sign of the occupants, and all around on the ground were enormous Tyrannosaurus foot prints.
"Uh-oh," said the first deputy. "I've seen this kind of thing before, and it isn't pretty."
"What is it?" the other deputy asked breathlessly.
"It's a car Rex."

What's a Carnosaurus's favorite dance?
The Fang Tango.

Where do the old Tyrannosaurus go when they retire?
To the Rex home.

What was a Carnosaurus's favorite dinner?
Stego and kidney pie.

What did the Tyrannosaurus say when he found the zoo?
"Oh, boy, a supermarket!"

A man who worked for a publishing house invented a time machine in his spare time. He transported himself back 200 million years and found himself surrounded by a tribe of hungry Tyrannosaurus.

"Who are you?" he cried.

"I'm the chief Tyrannosaurus," growled the biggest one. "Who are you?"

"I'm Fred, an editor."

"Well, Fred, I'm going to give you a promotion. You're about to become editor-in-chief."

Why did the Carnosaurus like eating the brains of his victims?
It gave him food for thought.

How did the Carnosaurus pray?
"Give us this day our daily dead."

What's the difference between a dinosaur and a salesman named Murray?
One's a giant reptile and the other's a gentile rep.

What's the difference between a butcher and a hungry Tyrannosaurus at Sizzler?
One weighs a steak and the other awaits a steak.

What's the difference between Santa Claus and an out-of-breath Triceratops?
Santa Claus wears a red suit. The Triceratops just pants.

What did the Tyrannosaurus have when it devoured its prey at noon?
Lunch meat.

Why do dinosaurs like molasses?
Because it's made from saurgum.

Why did the Tyrannosaurus stand on the watch?
Because it wanted to be on time.

What do you call two twenty-ton Titanosaurus having a chat?
A heavy discussion.

What have you got when your Tyrannosaurus is cross?
Tyrannosaurus Vex.

What kind of spell did the wizard use to make Timmy think he was a dinosaur?
A Tyrannosaurus Hex.

What is it called when two ferocious dinosaurs start kissing?
Tyrannosaurus Necks.

Doctor, doctor, my wife thinks she's a baby Diplodocus!
Well, tell her to grow up!

Did you hear about the dinosaur who caught a cold?
It turned into Brontochitis.

Which dinosaur wrote *Jane Eyre*?
Charlotte Bronto.

What did the Tyrannosaurus order at the fancy restaurant?
Stego Tartare.

What kind of dinosaurs lived in maples?
Treeceratops.

Which dinosaur was always the most fashionable?
The Trendceratops.

Which dinosaur played the most practical jokes?
The Trickceratops.

Which dinosaurs made the best judges?
The Trialceratops.

Which dinosaurs were always travelling?
The Tripceratops.

Where were most dinosaurs found?
Between their heads and their tails.

What's grey, has enormous claws, and weighs a hundred pounds?
An anorexic Tyrannosaurus.

How do you make dinosaur gegs?
You scramble some dinosaur eggs.

Leonardo da Vinci built a time machine and went back millions of years. He found himself being chased by a hungry Carnosaurus, so he took a drawing out of his pocket, wadded it up and threw it at the Carnosaurus.
It had an art attack.

Why didn't Gus the Goofasaurus do his homework?
He heard he was going to be extinct, so he didn't see the point.

SARAH: You know that cake I baked for you? A dinosaur ate it.
LEE: Oh no, that's terrible. There's nothing worse than a dinosaur with an upset stomach.

PATIENT: Dr. Freud, every night I dream that there are dinosaurs sitting on my bedposts, ready to jump down and eat me. What can I do?
DR. FREUD: Sharpen your bedposts.

LEONARD: When I was little, my mother told me that if I didn't stop pretending I was a dinosaur, I'd grow up to be an idiot.
BRIAN: Couldn't stop, huh?

MAN: Dr. Freud, you've got to help me. My son thinks he's a Tyrannosaurus. He crawls around the house all day on his hands and knees, growling. Yesterday he tried to bite the dog.
DR. FREUD: It's just a phase, he'll grow out of it.
MAN: Well, I don't like it, and neither do his wife and daughter.

TIMMY: Dr. Freud, my family sent me here because I like dinosaurs.
DR. FREUD: There's nothing wrong with that. I like dinosaurs.
TIMMY: Good. Why don't you come over to my house? I've got three hundred in my bedroom.

Why did the Brontosaurus name its baby Theophilus?
Because it was Theophilus baby it had ever seen.

Did you hear about the Pteranodon that swallowed a tapeworm?
It died by inches.

What about the Triceratops that was eaten by a giant snake?
It died by the foot.

How do you make an Ultrasaurus fly?
First you make it a great big zipper ...

What did the Tyrannosaurus say when it saw Santa Claus?
"Yum-yum."

BABY TYRANNOSAURUS: Look, I've eaten the whole Staurikosaurus family. I ate the mother and the two babies. Now I'm going to eat the pop.
MOTHER TYRANNOSAURUS: Put it down. You know that pop is bad for your teeth.

What weighs ten tons, is grey, has enormous teeth, and goes fifty miles an hour downhill?
A Tyrannosaurus on roller blades.

What do you call a long-necked dinosaur from Ontario?
A Toronto Bronto.

What did the Tyrannosaurus call the Triceratops Siamese twins?
A snack pack.

What would you get if you crossed a Diplodocus with a dozen eggs?
An omelette with a long neck.

What would happen if you crossed a Tyrannosaurus with a gazelle?
You'd get a quick bite.

What would you get if you crossed a Stegosaurus with a bluebird?
A blue-plate special.

What would you get if you crossed an Ultrasaurus with a hitchhiker?
A forty-ton pick-up.

The Tyrannosaurus burst into McDonald's and ate everyone in sight. "That's what I like about these fast-food places," it said. "They have the food ready as soon as you come in the door."

Why did the Carnosaurus fail math?
It subtracted the teacher.

What did the Tyrannosaurus say when he called the zoo?
"Do you deliver?"

ELAINE: Arnold, are you awake? There's a ferocious dinosaur in the living room.
ARNOLD: No. I'm asleep.

Why did the Tyrannosaurus give up boxing?
It didn't want to ruin its looks.

The Tyrannosaurus attacked the swank hotel, but it only ate the people staying in the cheapest single rooms.
How come?
It was trying to cut down on suites.

What happened to the dinosaur that fell down the well?
It kicked the bucket.

Why did the Saltasaurus put dinomite under its pancakes?
Because it wanted to blow its stack.

Why did the Pachysaurus have such a hard time driving the golf ball?
Because it didn't have a steering wheel.

Did you hear that Charles Schulz invited Gus the Goofasaurus to be a character in his cartoon strip?
Gus turned him down. He didn't want to work for Peanuts.

How are dinosaur catchers paid?
By the pound.

Did you hear about the Mussasaurus that cut its left side off?
It was all right.

Why did the Nodosaurus brush its teeth with gunpowder?
It wanted to shoot its mouth off.

Where did the Kotasaurus keep its sleeping pills?
In its knapsack.

What would you get if you crossed a demon with a dinosaur?
Something dinobolic.

What happened to the Brachiosaurus that ate a bushel of prunes?
It got dino-rhea.

Did you hear that Scientology started with the Stegosaurs?
Then they called it Dino-etics.

What was the prehistoric magazine with the biggest circulation?
Reader's Dino-gest.

Why did the Triceratops's dinner make it sick?
It wasn't dino-gestible.

What do you call a Pteranodon ambassador?
A dino-tary.

Did you hear about the Kritosaurus that went faster than the speed of sound?
It entered the fourth dino-mension.

Which sauropod wrote *Out of Africa*?
Isak Dinosen.

What sound did doorbells make in the Triassic period?
Dino-dong.

Who was the god of wine during the Cretaceous era?
Dinonysius.

How do you get an Iguanodon's phone number?
Call Dino-rectory Assistance.

What kind of blimps did they have in the Jurassic period?
Dino-rigibles.

Why didn't the dinosaur goalie stop the ball?
It thought that's what the net was for.

What do you do if a dinosaur sits down in front of you at the movies and you can't see the screen?
Just watch the dinosaur and laugh when it does.

Did you hear the one about the dinosaur that ate a box of shredded wheat?
I can only tell you a little at a time—it's a cereal.

Why didn't the dinosaur buy a pocket calculator?
It didn't have any pockets.

What happened to the camel that had its hump bitten off by a Tyrannosaurus?
It changed its name to Humphrey.

Why did the Allosaurus throw its watch?
It wanted to see time fly.

What was the Titanosaurus's favorite saying?
THINK BIG.

Why didn't the Tyrannosaurus care when its prey jumped off a cliff?
It wanted it dead or alive.

Why did the Goofasaurus buy a bicycle pump?
It wanted to cure its flat feet.

Why did the Tyrannosaurus feel sick after it ate the Nobel Prize-winning paleontologist?
Because you can't keep a good man down.

Why did the Triceratops wear bells around its neck?
Because its horns were broken.

Why did Erica put a dinosaur in Lynne's bed on her birthday?
Because she said she wanted a big surprise.

GREG: How do you spell blind dinosaur?
ERNIE: B-L-I-N-D D-I-N-O-S-A-U-R.
GREG: No, you spell it B-L-N-D D-N-O-S-A-U-R, because if it had those two Is it wouldn't be blind.

What does a Tyrannosaurus say to you to let you know it's hungry?
"Come here."

Did you hear about the Brontosaurus with the loud neck?
It had to wear a muffler.

What happened to the dinosaur when it was hit on the head with an apple?
It was shaken to the core.

Arnold called 911. "Help, come quickly," he cried.
"What's wrong?"
"The postman is up a tree, teasing my poor Tyrannosaurus Rex."

How did Arnold know when his pet Tyrannosaurus was happy?
It stopped biting him.

Why did the Ultrasaurus have holes in his pants?
How else could he get his legs through?

ELAINE: Does your Tyrannosaurus bite strangers?
ARNOLD: Only the ones it doesn't know.

TEACHER: Can anyone tell me where dinosaurs were found?
ELAINE: They were so big, how could anyone lose them?

MUSEUM GUIDE: We call that dinosaur a Lancangjiangosaurus.
ELAINE: Why?
MUSEUM GUIDE: Because it looks like a Lancangjiangosaurus, stupid.

Why did the Goofasaurus keep popping out of bed?
It plugged its electric blanket into the toaster by mistake.

Jody went to buy some wool to knit her Brontosaurus a scarf. The lady behind the counter said, "Maybe you should bring him down to the store so I can tell you how much yarn to buy."
"Oh, no," said Jody. "It's supposed to be a surprise."

PATIENT: Dr. Freud, I live with my brother, and he keeps seven dinosaurs in our apartment. They make a terrible mess and the smell is awful.
DR. FREUD: Maybe you should open some windows?
PATIENT: What? And let my Pteranodons escape?

ELAINE: What kind of skull is that?
MUSEUM GUIDE: That's the skull of a Longosaurus.
ELAINE: And what's the smaller skull next to it?
MUSEUM GUIDE: That's the skull of the same Longosaurus when it was a baby.

What did the ant say when the Titanosaurus stepped on it?
"Your feet are killing me."

Why was the Tyrannosaurus mad at Mother Nature?
She gave it an ugly look.

Did you hear about the dinosaur kleptomaniac?
He was taking something for it.

Did Stegosaurs get eaten by Tyrannosaurs very often?
Never more than once.

Why did Gus the Goofasaurus plant a field a mile long and six inches wide?
He wanted to grow spaghetti.

What happened to the Tyrannosaurus that swallowed a frog?
It croaked.

AUNT HAZEL: Billy, eat your spinach. It's good for growing boys.
BILLY: I don't want to grow boys. I want to grow dinosaurs.

When did the optometrist know that the dinosaur needed glasses?
As soon as it walked through the window.

Did you know that Alice beats her dinosaur up every morning?
She gets up at seven and it gets up at eight.

ELAINE: Does your dinosaur have fleas?
ARNOLD: Don't be silly. Dinosaurs don't have fleas; they have baby dinosaurs.

Do you know how long dinosaurs should be fed?
The same way as short ones.

Why didn't the Goofasaurus realize it was standing in quicksand?
It took a long time to sink in.

Why was the Goofosaurus nicknamed "Candy bar?"
He was half nuts.

Why did the Goofasaurus spend half his time trying to be witty?
He was a half-wit.

What happened when the Goofasaurus changed his mind?
It didn't work any better.

ELAINE: I sent my Tyrannosaurus to your store to get five pounds of hamburger. You only gave him two pounds. Did you even weigh that meat?
BUTCHER: Sure I weighed it. Have you weighed your dinosaur?

Suzie came home one cold wintry day to find her dinosaur sitting in front of a roaring fire. Why was she so upset?
Because she didn't have a fireplace.

FRED: Does your Tyrannosaurus have any brothers or sisters?
BARNEY: No, he's an only child.
FRED: Thank goodness.

FIRST TYRANNOSAURUS: What's that book you're reading?
SECOND TYRANNOSAURUS: It's called *How to Serve Your Fellow Dinosaur*.

LIBRARIAN: You'll have to take your dinosaur out of here. He's scaring the patrons, and they can't read.
PHYLLIS: That's terrible. I've been able to read since the first grade.

MARY: How did your Brontosaurus get a black eye?
HARRY: You see that telephone pole?
MARY: Yes.
HARRY: Well, he didn't.

SAM: I heard your Allosaurus swallowed a quarter. How is she?
PAM: No change yet.

Did anyone laugh when the Tyrannosaurus fell on the ice?
No, they were too scared. Only the ice made some cracks.

Why did Gus the Goofasaurus study the blotter?
He found it very absorbing.

How did Gus the Goofasaurus get a gleam in his eye?
He slipped when he was brushing his teeth.

Why did Gus the Goofasaurus leave after the first act of the play?
The program said "Second Act—one year later," and he couldn't wait.

What did Pteranodons use when they wanted to stop flying?
Air brakes.

What did the Tyrannosaurus say to his lunch's skeleton?
"It was nice gnawing you."

What did the Brontosaurus say to the adding machine?
"Can I count on you?"

Why did Gus the Goofasaurus use bananas for shoes?
He wanted a pair of slippers.

Why did Gus the Goofasaurus go to Texaco when he had a toothache?
He heard it was a filling station.

What do you call a friendly Tyrannosaurus?
A vegetarian.

MOTHER: Janey, stop making faces at that Tyrannosaurus.
JANEY: He started it.

Why did Gus the Goofasaurus quit his job at Dunkin' Donuts?
He got tired of the hole business.

What kind of bird did the Tyrannosaurus have in its throat?
A swallow.

Why couldn't Gus the Goofasaurus get a ticket to go to the moon?
The moon was full.

LARRY: I had to go to the doctor after the Tyrannosaurus bit me.
FELICIA: How was it?
LARRY: Hilarious.
FELICIA: Really?
LARRY: Sure, I was in stitches.

PAINTER: May I paint your dinosaur?
LOUISE: No, thanks, I like her this color.

Why did the Brontosaurus eat a hole in the rug?
She wanted to see the floor show.

HUBERT: Is ink expensive?
MOTHER: No.
HUBERT: Then why was Dad so upset when I fed some to my dinosaur?

Why didn't the Brontosaurus want to go up the street to eat?
He didn't like concrete.

ALICE: Did you know dinosaurs had six legs?
DAN: That's wrong. They only had four.
ALICE: No. They had forelegs in front and two in the back.

What's red and white on the outside and grey on the inside?
An inside-out dinosaur.

If you were being chased by a bull and a Tyrannosaurus, which one would you shoot first?
The Tyrannosaurus. You can always shoot the bull.

What happened when the Kansas City Brontos drove in a run to tie the game?
They evened the dinoscore.

Did you hear about the king of dinosaurs who found Excalibur?
It was his dinosword.

What did the Bronto use to paddle the boat?
A dino-oar.

What did they call dull Pteranodons?
Dino-bores.

What do you study if you're interested in prehistoric history?
Dino-lore.

What did linoleum cover in the Cretaceous period?
The dino-floor.

Who were homeless 200 million years ago?
The dino-poor.

What noise did the Tyrannosaurus make when it was angry?
A dino-roar.

What did the prehistoric peace treaty end?
The dino-war.

What kind of work did Sammy make his Stegosaurus do around the house?
Dino-chores.

What kind of business did Macy's run for Triceratops?
A dino-store.

Where did the Allosaurus go to play in the ocean?
To the dino-shore.

What do you get if you put a Bronto on graham crackers with chocolate and marshmallows?
A dino-s'more.

How do ferns make dinosaurs?
With dino-spores.

What do you get if you cross a dinosaur with a troll?
A monster that lives under bridges.

SCIENTIST 1: I've just discovered a method for growing wool on dinosaurs.
SCIENTIST 2: Doesn't that make the dinosaurs feel a little sheepish?

Did you hear about that cow that got into a fight with a Stegosaurus?
She was creamed.

What do you call a dinosaur from China?
A Sino-dino.

Did you hear about the white Triceratops with pink eyes?
It was an albino dino.

Why was the butcher worried the dinosaur would escape from his shop?
He had a big steak in him.

The Lizard of Oz

There once was a Bronto named Gus
Whose neck was as long as a bus
He got the mumps bad
Which sure made him mad
And boy, that dino could cuss.

Tongue Twisters

Say the following three times fast!

Rubber baby bronto buggy bumpers.

The sticky stocky stega sought six sick sardines.

Ten Tyrannosaurus tied together tried to trot to town Tuesday.

Mary had a Brontosaurus
Its neck was long and gray
And everywhere that Mary went
People ran away.

Little Miss Muffet
Sat on a tuffet
Feeding her dinosaur, Jim.
Along came a spider
And sat down beside her
And the dinosaur also ate him.

There once was a smart kid named Morris
Whose pet was a big Stegosaurus.
It ate his dad's car,
That hungry dinosaur.
Now Morris must buy a new Taurus.

A dino from far off lands
Had lots of time on its hands.
It went to the movie
And thought they were groovy.
So it started its own rock band.

A Rex named Tyrannosaur Fred
Ate lots of crackers in bed.
His mother said, "Fred,
You're messing the bed.
Why don't you eat people instead?"

An MTV DJ named Horace
Wanted a pet Brontosaurus.
He bought a big leash
and searched the Far East,
But the best that he found was a porpoise.

Terry had a Pterodactyl
Its wings were strong and true.
Every time it flapped the things,
A cold Nor'easter blew.

Hickory dickory dock
The Bronto ran up the clock.
The dino struck one—
and the clock fell down.
Hickory dickory dock.

Books About Dinosaurs

The Tyrannosaurus: Our Best Friend
  by Shirley U. Geste

Roping Dinosaurs
  by Larry Yett

Treating Dinosaur Bites
  by Dr. Hurry

Feeding Your Hungry Brontosaurus
  by Lottie Leaves

The Charge of the Tyrannosaurus
  by Ron Feryurlife

Five favorite dinosaur books:

Little Bo Dino
The Dino of Oz
Winnie the Dino
Dino Lox and the Three Bears
Dr. Dinolittle

Five favorite dinosaur TV programs:

Dino Knows Beast
The Dino Bunch
Dinanza
Saurfeld
Dino Women

Five favorite dinosaur movies:

The Lizard of Oz
Night of the Iguanodon
Dino at Eight
Home Allosaurus
A Saur is Born

Five great dinosaur actors:

Matthew Brontoick
Alan Aldasaurus
Marlon Bronto
Rex Harrison
Tyrann Power

Five great dinosaur actresses:

Ptery Garr
Dino Keaton
Saurus Day
Susan Saurandon
Dina Durbin

Tyrannosaurus, My Foot!

The lame-brained scientist was digging for fossils in the Mojave Desert. A team of respected professors came by to examine his finds.

"Well, well, young man," said Dr. Helena Handbasket. "It looks as if you've discovered a new dinosaur."

"Oh, no!" cried the scientist. "I wanted to find one that was at least 200 million years old!"

The work at the dinosaur dig was very hard. Hilary felt she was overworked, so she went to see her boss.

"Listen, I need a raise," she said. "I've been doing the work of three people for the last two years."

"I can't give you a raise," said Marvin. "But if you tell me who the other two people are, I'll fire them."

The movie theater was showing a film about prehistoric times. A tribe of cavemen had just captured a Brontosaurus and had tied it to the ground with lots of vines. They were about to build a fire and roast it alive when Mrs. Smith said to her husband, "Dear, do you think I should call home and see how the babysitter is getting along with the children?"

Joe was taking a class at the university on dinosaurs. The old professor was very cranky. "If there are any idiots in this class, please stand up."

There was a short pause; then Joe stood up.

"So you're an idiot?" snapped the professor.

"No, sir," said Joe. "I just didn't like to see you standing there all alone."

Kevin got a job as a longshoreman, unloading freight from ships. A freighter came in full of rare dinosaur bones and fossils, and as Kevin was walking down the gangplank with an Allosaurus femur under each arm, the plank gave way, and he fell into the water.

"Help, I can't swim!" he shouted as he surfaced the first time.

But nobody jumped in.

"Help!" he cried as he surfaced the second time.

But nobody helped.

He came up for the third time. "If somebody doesn't help me," he yelled, "I'm gonna let go of these bones!"

Two mother Maiasauras were guarding the nests where they had laid their eggs.

"It certainly was windy yesterday," said one.

"You're telling me," said the other. "It was blowing so hard that I laid the same egg five times."

Rhoda got a stuffed dinosaur for her birthday. She and Franny were playing in the family room, but Rhoda wouldn't let Franny even touch her new dinosaur. Finally Franny said, "If I got a dinosaur toy, I'd let you play with it."

"That's okay," said Rhoda. "I already have one."

An Oviraptor walked into a restaurant and said, "Do you serve rotten eggs?"

The waitress replied, "Sit down, we serve anyone."

Two geologists hired a guide to lead them to a remote part of Colorado where they were sure they would find new dinosaur fossils. The three of them walked and walked for days, until one geologist finally said, "Listen, we've passed that stream bed twice now in the last two days. You're leading us round in circles! I thought you were supposed to be the best guide in Colorado."

"I am!" retorted the guide. "Only now I think we're in Idaho!"

The insurance broker was furious with his associate. "You sold a million-dollar policy to a dinosaur!" he shouted. "We'll go broke paying that off."

"Don't worry," said the associate. "He told me he never goes more than a few miles from home."

"How's that going to help?"

"I looked at the census report, and it said that no dinosaurs have ever died in America."

Gus the Goofasaurus got an apartment all of his own. His landlord stopped by a few days later to see how it was going.

"I like it," said Gus. "Except those people downstairs bang on the pipes until two in the morning."

"Does that bother you?" asked the landlord.

"No, I'm usually up that late practicing my tap dancing."

The dinologist sailed to Saurasia, the last place where dinosaurs lived. He went to a clearing in the jungle, took out a violin, and began to play. Soon, the clearing was full of all kinds of dinosaurs, intently listening to his beautiful music.

Suddenly a Tyrannosaurus burst into the clearing and devoured the man, violin and all.

"What have you done?" a Triceratops cried. "How could you not be moved by that beautiful music?"

The Tyrannosaurus cocked its head and said, "Speak up. I've got a cold and I can't hear a thing."

Two Ankylosaurus were walking through the jungle when they found a third one unconscious on the ground. They managed to wake him after a few minutes.

"What happened?" they asked.

"Well, I was standing here talking to a Stegosaurus I just met, when all of a sudden he just hit me and I passed out."

"Can you describe this Stegosaurus?"

"That's what I was doing when he hit me!"

Gus the Goofasaurus was walking through the jungle dragging a vine behind him.

"What are you doing dragging that vine?" said Sally the Smartosaurus.

"Have you ever tried pushing one?"

The academic conference was going very badly. The young professors were all quite taken with new theories, and the older scholars wanted nothing to do with them.

One young woman got up to make a speech on her revolutionary theory of why dinosaurs became extinct. About two minutes after she had started, a grizzled looking old researcher stood up in the audience.

"This is ridiculous. You know absolutely nothing about the subject on which you are speaking. Why, I'd wager you don't even know how many toes a dinosaur had!"

The young professor smiled. "Why don't you take your shoe off and we'll count them!"

A month later Dr. Freud attended a meeting of the Psychiatric Association.

"How is your treatment of that fellow who thinks he's a Brontosaurus progressing?" asked Dr. Jung.

"I thought he'd snapped out of it," Dr. Freud said. "But now I'm not so sure."

"Why?"

"He just paid his bill in boulders."

An overeager vacuum-cleaner salesman called on Ms. Pteranodon in her cave. He threw a handful of cigarette butts and ashes on the floor and said, "If my vacuum cleaner can't pick up every last bit of that mess, I'll eat it!"

"Get started," said Ms. Pteranodon. "I don't have any electricity."

When Gus the Goofasaurus was going to dinosaur school, his mother sent this note to the teacher:

"Gus is a very sensitive dinosaur. If he misbehaves, just yell at the dinosaur next to him. That will be enough to scare Gus."

The third-grade class went on a field trip to the Natural History Museum to see the new dinosaur exhibit. On the bus on the way there, Andy said, "Keep your eyes closed the whole time. If we don't see anything, she can't give us a test on it."

Gus the Goofasaurus got another job, but he was so inept that the boss was bawling him out after just twenty minutes.

"I can't believe you could be so dumb," the boss shouted. "What's your IQ, anyway?"

Gus thought about it for a minute and said, "20-20?"

The missionary was walking through the jungle when he ran into a Tyrannosaurus Rex. He took off running, but he clearly wasn't fast enough. So he dropped to his knees and began to pray fervently for deliverance.

To his surprise, the Tyrannosaurus dropped down to its knees beside him.

"Gracious," said the missionary. "How wonderful to be praying with you. I was afraid for my life."

"Quiet," said the Tyrannosaurus. "I'm saying grace."

The hotel had advertised for a new bellhop. They required someone who was strong, experienced, and who could speak several languages, since they had many foreign guests. There was only one applicant, a Triceratops. His resume was quite impressive. He could lift the manager's desk with one foot, and he'd spent six years working at the Grand Hotel as a bellboy.

"I guess the only question I have to ask is what other languages you speak," said the manager.

"Oink," said the Triceratops. "Bow-wow. Cock-a-doodle-doo."

Two cavemen were sitting on a rock when a herd of Sauropods stampeded by.

"Wow!" said the first. "I wonder how many of them there were."

"Seventy-two," said the other.

"How do you know?"

"Easy. I counted the legs and divided by four."

Randy came home to find a Tyrannosaurus sitting in a tree in his front yard. He was so upset, he hardly knew what to do. He looked in the yellow pages, and to his surprise, he saw a listing for Dinosaur Removal Service.

He called up and the woman said, "I'll be right over."

In ten minutes her truck pulled up. She got out carrying a gun and leading a pit bull on a leash.

She handed Randy the gun. "This is a pretty simple affair. I'll climb the tree and tickle the Tyrannosaurus until he falls out. My pit bull here will rip out its throat, and then I'll just haul it away in my truck."

"Okay," said Randy. "But what do I do with the gun?"

"Oh," she said. "If I fall out of the tree, shoot the dog."

Leo had a big, vicious Tyrannosaurus that he was very proud of. He was always boasting that it could whip any dog in a fight. One day a little old lady knocked at his door.

"I'm sorry, sir," she said. "But I'm afraid my little dachshund has just killed your dinosaur."

"What!" Randy shouted. "How could a scrawny little dog like that kill my Tyrannosaurus? Just yesterday he beat up six Dobermans."

"He got caught in his throat."

A Triceratops was walking through the jungle with a bandage on his left horn.

"Wow," said a Diplodocus it met. "That must have been some fight."

"Oh, I wasn't in a fight," the Triceratops said. "I bit myself."

"That's impossible. How could you bite a horn on top of your head."

"Easy. I stood on a boulder."

A frisky little Stegoceras ran up to a great big Tyrannosaurus and gave her a big, sloppy kiss. Then he dashed off.

The furious Tyrannosaurus followed in hot pursuit.

The Stegocerus could tell that she was gaining on him. Just then, he saw a newspaper on the ground. He grabbed it, sat down on a rock, and pretended to read.

The Tyrannosaurus came running up. "Have you seen a lousy little Stegocerus run by here?" she shouted.

"You mean the one that kissed the Tyrannosaurus?" he asked.

"Oh, no!" she cried. "You mean it's in the newspaper already?"

Biff bought a Triceratops at the pet store. A few weeks later he called up and complained that the dinosaur's horns were ripping big holes in his walls.

"It's an easy problem to fix," said the lady in the store. "Just file down the horns, and they won't hurt anything."

The next day Biff was back at the pet store for another Triceratops.

"You must have solved that problem with the horns if you're ready for a second one," said the lady.

"Nope," said Biff. "I killed the last one when I put its head in the vise."

A hawk, a mountain lion, and a skunk were sitting in the forest discussing who was the most powerful.

"I am," claimed the hawk. "I swoop down on my prey unseen and break its back before it even knows what happened."

"No," snorted the mountain lion. "I am the most powerful. My claws are the sharpest in the land."

"Hah!" said the skunk. "All I have to do is wave my tail and everyone runs for cover."

Just then a Tyrannosaurus charged up and ate each of them ... hawk, lion, and stinker.

Jenny was having an awful time controlling her Staurikosaurus. It was always escaping and eating somebody's pet. One day she got a phone call.

"Are you the lady who owns the Staurikosaurus?"

"Yes," Jenny replied.

"Well, this is the ringmaster of the circus. I was leading twenty elephants down the street when your dinosaur charged up and attacked the last elephant in the line and knocked it clear across the street. Then he ate it."

"Oh, I'm so sorry," Jenny replied. "How much do I owe you?"

"One million dollars."

"One million dollars? That's outrageous. One elephant can't cost that much."

"No, an elephant only costs fifty thousand dollars. But when your dinosaur struck my elephant, the chain reaction pulled the tails out of the other nineteen elephants in line."

The caveman walked into the cave and threw a handful of sand on the ground.

"What are you doing?" said his wife.

"This is magic sand. It keeps dinosaurs away."

"Dummy, there aren't any dinosaurs here."

"See," he said. "It works."

Gus the Goofasaurus had just come back from Pennsylvania where he went to an amusement park called Dino Land. He was telling his friend about it.

"There are some great rides there," he said. "But the best thing is they named it after us."

"Really?" said his friend. "They call it Gus and Leroy's?"

Erica persuaded Lynne to go to a concert with her. The violinist was a Tyrannosaurus Rex. The music was so awful that many people held their hands over their ears. When the concert was over, no one applauded. In fact, many people booed.

Enraged, the Tyrannosaurus jumped into the audience. Everyone scrambled for an exit.

"I just hope," yelled Erica, "that his Bach is worse than his bite."

Ben was sitting in a park with his Tyrannosaurus when a man came walking by. "What's that?" the man exclaimed.

"That's my trained dinosaur," Ben explained. "Watch."

He took a sandwich out of his backpack and put it on the ground ten feet away. "Tyrannosaurus, my sandwich!" he said.

Instantly, the dinosaur jumped on the sandwich and ate it in one gulp.

"Boy," said the man. "Can I try?"

"Sure," said Ben.

The man took an apple out of his pocket and set it on the ground. "Tyrannosaurus, my apple!" he cried.

The dinosaur pounced, and the apple disappeared between his mighty jaws.

Just then a second man walked up.

"What the heck is that ugly thing?"

"It's my Tyrannosaurus," Ben replied.

The man scoffed and said, "Tyrannosaurus, my foot!"

"What do you do for a living?" said the man to the woman sitting next to him on the plane.

"Oh, I'm a dinosaur cleaner. I work at the zoo and everyday I climb into the dinosaurs' mouths and scrape their teeth clean."

"Good heavens," said the man. "How do you survive?"

"Oh, I do a little waitressing on the side."

Amy was having a banana split at the ice-cream parlor when an Allosaurus came in. It didn't say anything, but the waiter brought it a chocolate sundae. First it took the spoon out of the glass. Next it picked the cherry off the top, licked up the whipped cream, and poured the rest straight down its throat. Then it swallowed the glass as well, paid its bill, and walked out.

"I don't believe what I just saw," Amy said to the waiter.

"I know," the waiter replied. "Can you believe it? It always leaves the spoon. That's the best part."

A dinosaur comes into a coffee shop and sits down at the counter and orders a sandwich.

"Excuse me," says the waitress. "But just what are you?"

"I'm a Titanosaurus," the dinosaur replies.

"But I thought Titanosaurus were the biggest dinosaurs ever. Aren't you kind of small?"

"Well, you know what it's like. The newspapers always exaggerate."

A Martian and a Pteranodon walk into the same coffee shop the next day. "I'll have a Kryptonite sandwich," the Martian says.

"Golly," says the waitress. "I didn't think Martians could speak English."

"Hah! Fooled you!" laughs the Pteranodon. "I'm a ventriloquist."

A doctor, a dentist, and a lawyer are driving through the country when their car breaks down. They hike to the nearest farmhouse and call for a tow truck, but the truck can't come until the next day, so they ask the farmer to put them up.

"Okay," she says, "but I've only got one spare bed, so one of you will have to stay in the barn. But I'm warning you, I keep a Tyrannosaurus Rex out there."

The three draw straws, and the doctor loses. He goes out to sleep in the barn. A few minutes later there's a knock at the door, and they open it. The doctor is standing there, white as a sheet, and he says, "I'm sorry, but I just can't sleep in that barn. That dinosaur has me scared out of my wits."

So the dentist volunteers, and she goes out to the barn. A few minutes go by, and there's another knock at the door. When they open it, it's the dentist, holding her nose. "I'm sorry," she explains. "But that dinosaur stinks. I can't bear it."

This time, the lawyer agrees to go out to the barn. Three minutes go by and there's yet another knock at the door. They open it, and there's the Tyrannosaurus, as white as a sheet and holding its nose.

Marylin responded to an ad in the paper for a maid. When she got to the mansion, the butler pulled her aside. "Let me just tell you one thing. The master of this house is a Brontosaurus. He doesn't care if you think that's unusual, because he's proud of the fact that he's so much richer than all the other dinosaurs. But he is extremely sensitive about the fact that his ears are so small. Whatever you do, don't mention his ears."

Marylin nodded and went into the study for her interview.

Everything went very well. The Brontosaurus was quite impressed with Marylin's recommendations and her experience. Finally he asked, "Do you notice anything odd about me?"

"Well, yes, as a matter of fact I do. I don't often meet a dinosaur who wears contact lenses."

"Incredible," the dinosaur said. "I like your attention to details. How can you tell I'm wearing lenses?"

"Easy," said Marilyn. "You don't have any ears to hold up your glasses."

Sylvia ran into her old friend Andy on the street. "How's it going?" she asked.

"Oh, not so well," Andy said. "For the last two months I've been working at the circus. I'm in charge of cleaning out the dinosaur cages. I'm always dirty and I've been bitten seven times since I started."

"That's terrible," Sylvia sympathized. "You should quit."

"Quit?" Andy shouted. "And leave show business?"

Maude showed up for work an hour late.

"Where have you been?" shouted her boss.

"It was terrible. I was walking to work and a dinosaur jumped out of an alley, stole my purse, and gave me a big kiss!"

Her boss looked at her. "And that took an hour?"

For fifty years Rex the Tyrannosaurus had ruled the jungle. Every other dinosaur lived in terror of him. One day he finally died. Two hundred dinosaurs showed up for his funeral.

"It's amazing that so many would come to pay their respects to Rex," his widow sobbed, looking at the crowd.

"Well," said her sister. "Give people what they want and they'll show up."

The sheriff calls the posse together and says, "Fellas, three dinosaurs have escaped from the zoo. The first one weighs two tons, and there's a five thousand-dollar reward for catching it.

"The second one weighs five tons, and there's a ten thousand-dollar reward for catching it. The third one weighs ten tons and there's a twenty-five thousand-dollar reward for catching it. You will each receive a photo of the dinosaurs so you know what you're looking for. Any questions?"

A hand goes up in the back of the room. "Got anything that weighs twenty tons?"

Penny gets a phone call from her brother Doug. "I guess I should tell you what happened to me the other day. I was at the zoo and one of the Ceratosaurus escaped. First it bit off one of my ears, so now I don't hear so well. Then it bit off my other ear, and now I'm blind."

"Blind?" said Penny. "How come you're blind if you lost both your ears?"

"Because now my hat falls down over my eyes."

A crowd of people is waiting on the train platform, when all of a sudden, a Tyrannosaurus Rex comes running down the track.

"Don't panic," shouts a woman. "I'm from Oregon and this happens all the time. We just lie down and play dead and we're safe."

Everybody drops to the ground except one man. The hungry dinosaur comes closer and closer. Finally the man yells, "I'm from California. What do *I* do?"

Gus the Goofasaurus finally got a wagon. He was telling Sally the Smartasaurus about it.

"I was walking down the path, and suddenly the wagon started to go thump, thump, thump. So I stopped and put a new tire on. But as soon as I started, it went thump, thump, thump again."

"You know, the chances of two flat tires at once are extremely rare," Sally said.

"I know," said Gus. "But the first time I changed the wrong tire."

At summer camp, two young friends meet again. "Boy," says Marvin, "were your parents mad when you got sent home last year after putting itching powder in the director's sleeping bag?"

"Mad?" says Ernie. "Let me tell you about how mad they were. Just a week ago I was walking through the woods when a giant Tyrannosaurus jumped out of a tree and started to chase me. I ran and I ran and I finally escaped by hiding in a tiny cave until it went away."

"What does that have to do with how mad your parents were?"

"Because," sighed Ernie. "That was the first time in a year that I stopped thinking about how much my bottom still hurt."

George went out dinosaur hunting. He'd only been in the jungle about an hour when the game warden stopped him and asked to see his license. "Hey," says the warden. "You can't hunt dinosaurs with a license from last year."

"Don't worry about it," George replies. "I didn't catch any last year either."

The dictator was showing a group of diplomats around his palace. They came to a deep pit full of voracious dinosaurs. "This," snarled the dictator, "is where I test the will of anyone who disagrees with me. I throw them into the pit, and if they can make it to the other side and climb out, I give in to whatever they ask for. Except that no one has ever made it." And he laughed wickedly.

Suddenly the Canadian ambassador was diving into the pit. He hit the ground and rolled, just escaping a vicious bite from a Tyrannosaurus. He dashed madly for the other end of the pit, ducking under the dinosaurs' bellies and losing the sleeve off his jacket in the process. Fast as a bug he scrambled up the edge of the pit.

The other diplomats burst into applause. The dictator was very impressed. "Very good, my friend. For that I will do whatever you ask."

"Just one thing," panted the Canadian. "Tell me who pushed me!"

The phone rang at the front desk of the very expensive hotel. "This is Donald Trunk in room 2000. In exactly one hour I want you to send up a Tyrannosaurus wearing a green top hat, a Brontosaurus in ice skates, and a Triceratops that speaks French, Italian, and Hindu."

"Certainly, Mr. Trunk," said the clerk. Everyone in the hotel rushed around trying to get everything the billionaire wanted. After an hour had gone by the clerk called Donald Trunk back.

"We have a Tyrannosaurus wearing a green top hat, and a Brontosaurus in ice skates. We couldn't find any Triceratops that spoke Hindu, but we did find a Stegosaurus that is fluent in all three languages you requested. Will that do?"

"Of course not!" snapped Donald Trunk. "Just send me up a peanut-butter-and-jelly sandwich instead."

The next morning Mr. Trunk walked into a bakery. "I need a cake in the shape of a dinosaur," he said.

"I can have it for you at lunch time," said the baker.

At lunch Donald Trunk came back and the baker showed him the cake.

"No! No!" Trunk shouted. "That's a Brontosaurus. I wanted a Pteranodon."

"All right," sighed the baker. Come back in two hours."

Two hours later Trunk was back just as the baker finished the cake. Trunk took one look at it again and screamed, "Wrong again! I hate chocolate. It has to have cherry frosting."

"Okay, give me another hour," moaned the weary baker.

Another hour went by and Donald Trunk returned. This time he looked at the cake and said, "Perfect!"

"Good," says the baker, "I'll wrap it up for you."

"Don't bother," Trunk replies. "I'll eat it here."

Two cavemen are walking across the plains when they come across another with his head pressed to the ground. "Thirty-two Titanosaurs, ten males, fifteen females, seven hatchlings, heading south," the man says.

"Amazing!" says the first caveman. "You can tell all that just by listening to the ground?"

"No," the man moans. "They ran me over."

The Ceratosaurus is walking up and down the aisle of the grocery store. Finally it picks up a jar of peanut butter and approaches a clerk.

"Excuse me. Is this stuff any good for dry skin?"

"No, sir. That's peanut butter. Let me show you." And the clerk opens the jar, scoops some peanut butter out on a piece of celery, and gives it to the Ceratosaurus.

The dinosaur eats it, and a light goes on in its eyes. "Hey, you know, this stuff would go great in Chinese sesame noodles."

Ellen is walking through the forest when she meets an Ankylosaurus. "Gracious," says Ellen. "I didn't think there were any dinosaurs left in the world."

"Of course there are," says the dinosaur. "I'm Betty. Everybody knows me."

"I don't think so," says Ellen.

"Come on, I'll show you," says Betty.

So they walk into town to the fanciest hotel. Betty picks up a house phone and makes a call. In a few minutes one of the elevator doors opens and Madonna comes out. She runs over and gives Betty a big hug.

"Wow, I guess you're right," says Ellen. "I'm sorry I doubted you."

"That's nothing," says Betty. She makes another phone call, and in twenty minutes a helicopter lands outside the hotel. Betty and Ellen get in and are whisked to Washington, D.C. Bill and Hillary and Chelsea Clinton are waiting on the lawn, waving as the helicopter lands. Hillary feeds them some cookies and Bill and Betty tell some jokes.

"I'm sorry I doubted you," Ellen apologizes again as they walk away from the White House.

"Think nothing of it," Betty tells her. "I'll see you around."

Ellen walks a block when all of a sudden there is the sound of trumpets. She turns around to see the heavens open up directly above Betty, and a choir of angels descends, followed by an old man in a white beard and golden robes. A crowd gathers to watch, and one man turns to Ellen and says, "Hey, who's that guy talking to Betty?"

A mother and her son are riding their horses to market when suddenly a dinosaur jumps out from behind a tree.

"Okay, lady," it says. "Give me those dozen eggs you were carrying."

"I'm sorry, sir, but as you can see, I'm not carrying any eggs," the mother says carefully.

The dinosaur snarls and turns to the boy. "Alright, sonny. Hand over that catfish you caught."

"I'm not carrying any catfish," the boy says carefully, holding out his hands.

The dinosaur snarls again, then jumps on the horse and rides off.

"That was a close call," says the mother. "But I know you were carrying that catfish when we left home."

"I was, Mother, but I hid it in my mouth," the boy says. And he draws the catfish out of his mouth. "That's why I was talking funny."

"I know what you mean," his mother says. "That's where I hid my eggs." And one by one she spits out the dozen eggs into her apron.

Then she sighs. "If only your father were here. Then we could have saved the horse."

Buffy gets a job at the zoo feeding the animals. Her boss is showing her around, and they come to the cage where the Tyrannosaurus are kept.

"We feed them tortillas and pancakes," her boss explains.

"I didn't know dinosaurs liked tortillas and pancakes," Buffy said.

"They don't. But that's the only food we can slip under the door."

Mr. Fuddy went into the restaurant. "Waiter," he said, "do you have dinosaur legs?"

The waiter burst into tears.

"What's the matter?" Mr. Fuddy asked.

"How could you ask me a question like that?" the waiter sobbed. "You don't have to make fun of me just because I'm bow-legged."

Erica persuaded Lynne to go to another concert. A Stegosaurus came out and started to bang his head against a piano keyboard.

"What's he *doing*?" hissed Lynne.

"Why, he's playing by ear!" said Erica.

Traveling in the jungles of the Amazon, Victoria captured a rare Chickenosaurus, the missing link between dinosaurs and birds. She packed it up in a crate and eagerly sent it to Professor Siddons for examination.

A week later she sent him a fax from Brazil: "How's the Chickenosaurus?"

The fax came back: "Delicious!"

The Stegosaurus had been running and running, but it couldn't escape the hungry Velociraptor. Finally, it was caught.

"Any last words?" growled the voracious monster.

"Can I sing a song?" asked the Stegosaurus.

"Okay," growled the Velociraptor.

"One million bottles of beer on the wall, one million bottles of beer, if one of those bottles should happen to fall, ninety-nine thousand nine hundred ninety-nine bottles of beer on the wall . . ."

The M.C. stood up in front of the audience and said, "Ladies and gentlemen, tonight it is my pleasure to introduce to you the most famous Tyrannosaurus trainer in the world. For thirty years he has been sticking his right arm all the way down the throat of hundreds of these terrifying beasts. Just last week he retired and he's here to tell us all about his career. Ladies and gentlemen, I give you Lefty Monahan!"

The Stegosaurus was new in this part of the jungle. All the other dinosaurs told him, "Life's pretty good around here, but if anyone ever tells you that Fang is coming, run for your life. He's the biggest, meanest, ugliest Tyrannosaurus that ever walked the earth."

A few weeks went by when suddenly the cry rang through the jungle: "Fang is coming."

The Stegosaurus took off running, but pretty soon he heard thunderous footsteps behind him. He looked back and saw the biggest, meanest, ugliest looking Tyrannosaurus he could imagine following him. He knew he was doomed.

It wasn't very long before the Tyrannosaurus caught him. It picked him up in his teeth and shook him from side to side. It threw him into a tree and then started to kick him. Suddenly it stopped and turned away.

"Aren't you going to eat me?" the Stegosaurus whimpered in relief.

"Heck, no," the Tyrannosaurus replied. "Fang's coming. I've gotta get out of here."

Two Allosaurus were walking through the jungle when one got stuck in a tar pit. It struggled and struggled, but it couldn't get free from the ooze.

Suddenly it noticed its friend walking away.

"Hey," it shouted. "Don't leave me here."

"Don't worry," said the other. "Oil be seeing you."

Andy was always making up big stories to tell his friends. His sister Ann was getting pretty tired of it. One day on the school bus, Andy said, "I was at the beach the other day when a ferocious Tyrannosaurus came along and started chasing everyone away. Except me. I grabbed my sand bucket, filled it with water, and threw it in the dinosaur's face. Then it left everybody alone."

No one would believe his story, and one girl said to Ann, "That didn't really happen, did it?"

"Yes, it did," Ann smiled. "Afterward I went up and petted the dinosaur and fed it some candy. Believe me, its face was wet."

John sent Mary a letter telling her that he was breaking off their engagement. He told her she could keep the ring, but she should send back the picture of himself that he'd given her.

Mary was so mad that she went out and bought a book of dinosaur paintings. She cut each of them out and mailed them to John. Her note said: "Dear John, please pick your picture out of this pile and send the others back. I've forgotten what you look like."

There was an earthquake where Sam lived. Because he was worried about his pet Tyrannosaurus, he sent it to his parents to take care of until the aftershocks were over.

Two days later he got a telegram: Returning your dinosaur. Will trade for earthquake.

The dumb Tyrannosaurus finally caught a Triceratops. He was dragging it through the jungle by the tail, but its horns kept getting caught on everything. Finally he passed another Tyrannosaurus.

"Let me give you a hint," said the second Tyrannosaurus. "If you drag it by its head, the horns won't snag on things. It'll be much easier."

"Gee, thanks," said the stupid Tyrannosaurus. He picked up the head and started walking. An hour later he realized he was back where he'd started.

Two Tyrannosaurus were walking through the jungle when they came across the kind of scale that also gives you a fortune. The first one stood on it and out popped a little card. The second one looked at it. "It says you're handsome, charming and well-liked. And darned if it didn't get your weight wrong, too."

Terry tried as hard as he could to teach his Oviraptor to talk, but the only thing the dinosaur would say was, "Who is it?"

One day everyone was out and there was a knock at the door. "Who is it?" screeched the Oviraptor.

"It's the plumber," came the reply.

"Who is it?" said the dinosaur again.

"It's the plumber!" yelled the man outside.

"Who is it?" the dinosaur repeated.

"IT'S THE PLUMBER!" the poor man cried. But the frustration was so bad that he burst a blood vessel, had a stroke, and died on Terry's front porch.

When Terry came home he saw the dead man in front of the door. "Goodness," he said. "Who is it?"

"It's the plumber," said his dinosaur.

The zookeeper was driving a truckload of dinosaurs to a special exhibit. Along the way they stopped at a Wendy's. He went to the manager and said, "All these dinosaurs will want to pay for their lunches with pebbles. Don't worry about it. That's just a system we have at the zoo. When we're through, I'll settle up with you for the whole bill."

The manager agreed, and the seven dinosaurs came in. They ate fifty-two burgers, twenty-one bowls of chili, and thirty-five shakes. When they were done they cleaned up neatly after themselves and went back out to the truck.

"Now, about that bill," said the zookeeper. "Can you break a boulder?"

Penny was walking down the street when she saw a boy dressed in black walking behind two hearses and leading a Tyrannosaurus on a leash. Behind the boy was a line of a hundred kids.

Penny went up to the boy and said, "What's going on?"

"You see this dinosaur," the boy said. "I took him to school one day, and when Bob the bully attacked me, my dinosaur killed him. Then the principal tried to give me a spanking, and my dinosaur killed her too."

Penny thought about it, then said, "Can I borrow your dinosaur?"

"Okay," said the boy. "But get in line like everybody else."

Mr. and Mrs. Dinosaur hatched three eggs. "I'm going to call the first one Hot and the second one Cold," said Mrs. Dinosaur.

"Those are terrible names," said Mr. Dinosaur. "You can't call the children Hot and Cold."

"Yes, I can," retorted Mrs. Dinosaur. "I laid those eggs and I guarded them, so I can call them whatever I want."

"I'll give in," said Mr. Dinosaur. "On one condition. I get to name the third one."

"That's fair," said his wife. "You did have something to do with it. What do you want to call him?"

"Luke."

The Waxmans were on a tour of an ancient ruined city. Their guide took them to a great stadium where he said that the people who lived in the city would watch warriors fight ferocious dinosaurs.

"In that room over there, the warriors would dress for their battles," the guide said.

"How did anyone dress to fight a dinosaur?" Mr. Waxman asked.

"Very slowly," replied the guide.

Two Tyrannosaurus were going down a narrow path in the jungle from opposite directions. They met and neither could pass.

"I never back up for stupid idiots," said the first one.

"I always do," said the other, as it started walking backwards.

Seymour had a Ceratosaurus that he was very fond of. He took a trip to Florida, and after a week he called home to ask his brother how things were going.

"Mother's dead," his brother told him.

"What a shocking way to tell me," Seymour complained. "You should have broken it to me gently. You should have told me today that Mother had a cold. Then the next time I called you could have told me it was pneumonia. And then the third time I called I would have been prepared for this awful news. By the way, how's my Ceratosaurus?"

"Oh," said his brother. "I guess you should know it has a cold."

The Brontosaurus went into the restaurant and ordered a leaf salad without ranch dressing.

The waiter came back and said, "I'm sorry, we're out of ranch dressing. Would you like your salad without Roquefort?"

John opened the door to find a strange man standing there. "I'm the dinosaur trainer," the man said. "I've come to train your dinosaur not to run all over the neighborhood."

"But I didn't send for you," John protested.

"No," said the trainer. "Your neighbors did."

"Two dinosaurs have just escaped from the zoo. One stands twenty feet tall and the other slinks along at just four feet. Do not be alarmed. The police are hunting for them high and low."

And coming to a bookstore
near you in January 1994...

1,001 MORE DINOSAUR JOKES FOR KIDS

by Alice Saurus

Where does a Tyrannosaurus
sit in a movie theater?
Wherever he wants!

*Keep your friends and family
laughing through
those long winter nights.*

Published by Ballantine Books.

Knock-knock.
Who's there?
Summer.
Summer who?
Summer good, some are bad, but all of these jokes are guaranteed fun!

Published by Ballantine Books.

Call toll free 1-800-733-3000 to order by phone and use your major credit card. Please mention interest code KCF-493 to expedite your order. Or use this coupon to order by mail.

__500 WACKY KNOCK-KNOCK JOKES	345-38080-0	$3.99
__500 WILD KNOCK-KNOCK JOKES FOR KIDS	345-38159-9	$3.99
__1001 DINOSAUR JOKES FOR KIDS	345-38496-2	$3.99
__OH NO! NOT ANOTHER SIMPLE FAMILY JOKE BOOK	345-34035-3	$3.95
__1,000 CRAZY JOKES FOR KIDS	345-34694-7	$4.99
__1,000 JOKES FOR KIDS OF ALL AGES	345-33480-9	$4.99
__1,000 KNOCK-KNOCK JOKES FOR KIDS	345-33481-7	$4.99
__1,000 MORE JOKES FOR KIDS	345-34034-5	$4.99

Name_____
Address_____
City_____State_____Zip_____
Please send me the BALLANTINE BOOKS I have checked above.
I am enclosing $_____
  plus
Postage & handling* $_____
Sales tax (where applicable) $_____
Total amount enclosed $_____

*Add $2 for the first book and 50¢ for each additional book.

Send check or money order (no cash or CODs) to Ballantine Mail Sales, 400 Hahn Road, Westminster, MD 21157.

Prices and numbers subject to change without notice.
Valid in the U.S. only.
All orders subject to availability.   KCF-493